I WILL ARISE!
AND OTHER PLAYS

I WILL ARISE!

And Other Plays

by

T. B. MORRIS

LONDON
FREDERICK MULLER LTD.
29 Great James Street, W.C.1

FIRST PUBLISHED BY FREDERICK MULLER, LTD.
IN 1948
PRINTED IN GREAT BRITAIN BY WYMAN & SONS LTD.
LONDON, READING AND FAKENHAM

822

FOREWORD

THE six one-act plays included in this volume have been selected for their appeal to the imaginative producer. All may be presented in simple curtain settings, or with considerable elaboration. Each, in a different way, is a challenge alike to the producer and players who are looking for something out of the ordinary.

I Will Arise ! was specially written for presentation in the ruins of Coventry Cathedral, and was first produced there by Mr. E. Martin Browne. In the same week *Rain in Majorca* won the New Play Prize and the Drama section of the Coventry Festival. *Spanish Rhapsody* also had its first presentation at Coventry. *If Imagination Amend Them* scored high marks at Welwyn Drama Festival. The two remaining plays have not previously been offered for production, but *The Ribs of Argo* tied for second place among one hundred and eighteen entries in the Poetry Society's Drama Competition, 1946.

CONTENTS

	page
I WILL ARISE !	1
SPANISH RHAPSODY	41
IF IMAGINATION AMEND THEM	81
THE WHITE HORSEMAN	121
THE RIBS OF ARGO	165
RAIN IN MAJORCA	205

T. B. MORRIS

I Will Arise!

A Play in One Act

LONDON
FREDERICK MULLER LTD.
29 Great James Street, W.C.1

FIRST PUBLISHED BY FREDERICK MULLER, LTD.
IN 1948
PRINTED IN GREAT BRITAIN BY WYMAN & SONS LTD.
LONDON, READING AND FAKENHAM

DEDICATED

TO THE PEOPLE OF COVENTRY

SETTING AND PRODUCTION NOTES

FOR the purpose of stage direction, the setting is imagined as follows, though it may be adapted to any circumstances. Varying stage levels are advisable for effective grouping. A wall or curtain rises at the back of the stage, and against it centrally is an altar, behind which is a great wooden cross, which has fallen and is resting obliquely on one of its arms. This is the highest level; if possible steps lead down from it to the next level, the main stage. A still lower level, with steps leading up to the main stage, will greatly help in Chorus movements. If platforms and/or steps are not available, rostra and blocks of masonry should be used to raise the principal characters. Broken pillars and arches may soar above the heads of the players, though these may be left to the imagination helped by the text. If it is desired to add colour to the setting, a large banner or hanging may droop across the back wall as if half fallen from its original position, or a broken window still containing coloured glass may appear above the altar.

Entrances R. and L. upstage, or in the back wall for Michael and Lucifer. Further entrances R. and L. downstage for the other characters, if preferred, though it will be most effective if they can enter from the front through the audience.

Dramatic production in or near a church imposes a certain restraint upon action, and what there is must be stylized. Reverence and dignity are essential keynotes, and every movement and gesture must be made with these facts in mind. Yet there must be nothing either stodgy or sanctimonious in such a production, and, where it is necessary for characters to express evil, levity or humour, some relaxation to this end of the general tone must be

3

permitted to provide that contrast without which no drama can live. Something of the ballet, however restrained, should enter into the movements of the characters in this play. The groups of the Chorus must be deliberately posed to a statuesque stillness, yet must be fluid and frequently changed to accord with the moods of the play, all groups being built up with a view to obtaining the greatest pictorial effect, and movement changes rehearsed to a synchronized perfection. If the performance takes place in daylight, and therefore without the considerable aid of stage lighting, special attention is necessary to make-up and to getting all possible advantage out of colour, variation of grouping, and background music. Any previously known conditions of light and shadow in a building should be borne in mind in planning the grouping and movement of characters where stage lighting is not used. The essential quality of attack in ordinary stage productions is even more essential here. Nothing must be allowed to drag. Verse, even of a mournful and introspective nature, must be attacked and moved along, as well as kept vital by constantly changing levels. The verse in this piece is varied in metre to assist to this end. I have broken up the Chorus lines in places for six individual speakers. This is because a single voice is clearer and more effective than several together, and the change of solo speakers provides constant lift. Where lines are set for half or the whole of the Chorus to speak together, they must be rehearsed until they can be spoken without that raggedness which often mars choral verse. All players must be vital throughout, and this should be remembered all the time by those who have to remain still for longish periods without speech. They must keep their attention alive upon the other players where directed, and, by remaining still except for the stylized reactions directed by the Producer, always make their full contribution to the stage picture as a whole. There must be no undirected movement or gesture in any of the players.

Michael and Lucifer, though contrasted in appearance (preferably a fair Michael and dark Lucifer), should both be tall and beautiful. Great wings of conventionalized

4

shape will of course improve their appearance, but, even if these are obtainable, it may be found impossible to use them unless the players are far more static than is here directed. In this case, they should rely for their appearance on robes of rich and heavy material (together with armour if desired) and on their bearing. Michael's robes (and armour) should be white and silver or gold, Lucifer's red and black. If it cannot be arranged to fill these parts with players taller than the rest, they should occupy as often as possible heights above the other players.

The Architect should wear late fourteenth century costume, the Pilgrims early fifteenth century, the latter being considerably varied as to rank if there are a number of them. It will be observed that the first three Pilgrims have been given something of individuality, while the first three Citizens have not and may therefore be cast at pleasure. The Young Woman and Young Man are quite simple, ordinary people, and they might most effectively be dressed in military and Air Force uniform. It does not matter which wears which, but they should not be above junior officer rank. No head-dresses, of course, will be worn by men of any period. While it would be proper for the Pilgrims to cross themselves in the Cathedral, this action may be omitted if the performance is taking place in a Church of England or Nonconformist building. The dress of the Citizens may be modern, or of some fantastic " timeless " style.

The Pilgrims and Citizens may be groups of any convenient number of men and women and young people above about six or seven of each Pilgrims and Citizens. The largest available number that may effectively be grouped should be used, even though some of them remain silent.

A study of ballet " stills " will be of great value in working out the varied grouping and poses of the Chorus, especially in the stylized use of arms.

T. B. M.

THE CHARACTERS

PROLOGUE.

FIRST CITIZEN
SECOND CITIZEN
THIRD CITIZEN } *the modern half of the Chorus.*
OTHER CITIZENS

LUCIFER, *the Dark Angel.*

MICHAEL, *the White Angel.*

FIRST PILGRIM
SECOND PILGRIM
THIRD PILGRIM } *the medieval half of the Chorus.*
OTHER PILGRIMS

THE ARCHITECT.

THE YOUNG WOMAN.

THE YOUNG MAN.

THE SCENE

A ruined Cathedral.

I Will Arise! was first presented in the ruins of Coventry Cathedral on the afternoon and evening of Sunday, 18th June, 1944, by the Drama Committee of the Coventry Sports and Social Association in conjunction with the Cathedral Authorities, with an anonymous cast of twenty-one players.

The play was produced by E. Martin Browne.

6

I WILL ARISE!

PROLOGUE

(This, if desired, may be spoken by the ARCHITECT *before he changes into his medieval costume.)*

Lend your imagination, now, that we
May set our scene.   Here is a wreck of stone
Where once great beauty burned.   All overthrown
Lies the high cross ; the antique tracery
Of carven wood and gilding, gone.   And see
How empty gape the windows.   Toward the vault
Of a quiet Heaven the broken pillars halt
Like prayers of men who pray but dolefully.

Lend more than your imagination.   You
In this dark ruin have, with us, your part.
Shattered cathedral, devastated heart,
What are they but the same ?   There goodness grew
Where now is desolation.   Not alone
Come they who mourn, for you with them are one.

I WILL ARISE !

[*Music—a solemn march or lament—begins as the Prologue ends. The* CITIZENS *enter slowly, with bowed heads, either through the audience or else somewhere downstage, and group themselves on the lowest level of the stage in attitudes of mourning. Some are kneeling, some crouching, some standing with bowed heads. The music stops.*

1ST CITIZEN. To a dark place we have come
    And in a dark hour——

CITIZENS. To a ruined cathedral, symbolizing the ruin
    of ourselves ; of our lives and hopes,
    The ruin of our world.

1ST CITIZEN. Out of a dark place we make our prayer——

2ND CITIZEN. Or what passes with us for prayer——

1ST CITIZEN. But who—now—shall hear us ?

2ND CITIZEN. Who—now—shall give heed to us,
    Who are born under a bitter star ?

3RD CITIZEN. Who is there now to hear us ?

1ST CITIZEN. Are there ears toward the voices that
    mourn ;
    Mourn the passing of good,
    Of good from ourselves, of good from the world
    of man ?

2ND CITIZEN. We mourn the passing of good,
    Yet we have let it pass with little hindrance——

3RD CITIZEN. We who have shrivelled our souls in the
    pleasure and pain of worldly things
    And so come to desolation.

I WILL ARISE !

CITIZENS. Our souls are withered ; our souls are driven
like withered leaves in the winds of Hell.
For, though we have not forgotten that we ought to
pray,
We have lost the power and the direction of the
prayer.
We have lost faith in prayer.

[*The* CITIZENS *rise and lift their heads. The voices of the
speakers lift and become more rapid and urgent, each following
quickly upon the other.*

1ST CITIZEN. Not always have we known this darkness
and pain.
We have had youth and joy—joy in the wine of
our blood
And joy in the urge of creation ; the gold of the
morning
When hope was a loved playmate——

2ND CITIZEN. This we have known of promise
And warmed to the goal of achievement, seeing
ourselves
As those who lift and soar up and over the common
things
Into a broad perfection——

1ST CITIZEN.   Out and up
Into the wider blue of the infinite space
Light-decked with myriad worlds——

3RD CITIZEN.   Out and up and beyond
The little bonds of existence——

1ST CITIZEN.   Into the gaze of God !

CITIZENS. This we have known of promise.
This we have learned to read of the purpose of
God ;
The purpose of God towards man, writ fair in
the eyes of God.

[*They return to their attitudes of mourning.*

1ST CITIZEN. But what shall become of us now,
Who, seeing the light, have chosen the dark again
and again ?

9

3RD CITIZEN.   Who have fallen into the ultimate sin, the loss of our faith.

2ND CITIZEN.   Who suffer the ultimate punishment, loss of all hope.

3RD CITIZEN.   We have turned our eyes from the purpose of God for all men
To the baser purpose of every man for himself.

1ST CITIZEN.   And so we are come to the dark.   Our words are arrows
Sped towards nothing, falling back on ourselves.

CITIZENS.   Sped towards nothing—nothing.

[*A roll of thunder, or brief burst of discordant music.* LUCIFER *bounds on upstage L., with his drawn sword in his hand.*

LUCIFER (*in a great voice, terribly*).   Chaos ! Will God create again a world out of chaos ?   (*He spreads his arms wide, indicating the ruin about him.   More thunder.*)   See what I have done to your world !   I am Lucifer, lord of your broken world !   Civilization is broken to bits ! War ! Pestilence ! Famine ! The Devil comes into his own !

[LUCIFER *laughs hugely and moves downstage. The* CITIZENS, *who have shrunk back from him with a concerted gasp of fear, start back farther as he menaces them.   Then he laughs again, changes his tone to one of cynical tolerance, and addresses them more intimately.*

I invented a very nice line in sins—seven deadly ones and lots of others—oho, lots of little others !   And you took to them all and made some more for yourselves.   You've done the work of Hell very nicely—very nicely, thank you !   And now the world is shattered !   Humanity is done !   Chaos has come again !

[LUCIFER *regards the* CITIZENS, *enjoying their fear.* MICHAEL *enters quietly upstage R. and stands on the highest level, to R. of the altar.   He wears a sheathed sword, but his hands are bound before him with a scarlet band.* LUCIFER, *who has not seen* MICHAEL, *goes on talking to the* CITIZENS, *now in quite a friendly tone.*

But don't let me frighten you. There's no need for
alarm. Chaos is a comfortable state of muddle—if you
look at it that way—and the muddle-headed world will
love it. And don't worry about loss of faith. You
don't need faith. You've only to obey me.

MICHAEL (*in a ringing, beautiful voice*).   Lucifer !
    [LUCIFER *starts round with a hiss of fear, half-crouching,
his sword ready against attack. Then he sees that* MICHAEL
is bound, and laughs. The CITIZENS *also start round to face*
MICHAEL, *wondering.*

LUCIFER (*amused*).   How now, Michael !
    How do you like your bondage—ha ?
    [LUCIFER *moves up towards* MICHAEL, *still in a half-
crouching attitude, as though about to spring at him, but*
MICHAEL *remains straight and still.*

MICHAEL (*calmly*).   I see
    You have forgot that day in the world's dawning
    When, from the ultimate pinnacle of Heaven
    I threw you down.
    [LUCIFER *shrinks back a little.*

                                        You have forgotten
    How all the sons of morning drove your hosts
    Athwart the firmament, and cast you out
    From star and further star, through dizzy ages
    Of light and vast cerulean space, until
    We'd rid the heavens of pride.

LUCIFER (*recovering, straightening himself, challenging*).
                                My pride ! Ay, pride
    Such as you'd have, could you dare stand for your-
        selves
    And outface God, as I did. (*Proudly.*) Lucifer !
    Erstwhile son of the morning. Lord of night !
    Lord of mine own dominion ! Better state
    Than mopping and mowing at the Throne of Grace
    As you do, Michael.

MICHAEL (*terribly*).   There is no Throne of Grace
    For you and those who fell with you. It is written
    That we shall strive again——

LUCIFER. Then loose your hands,
You whom the sins of earth have bound.

[LUCIFER *springs near* MICHAEL *to menace him with his sword, but* MICHAEL *faces him calmly and again* LUCIFER *shrinks back.*

MICHAEL. My bondage
Is irksome, no denying. An archangel
Not gladly suffers this indignity.
Yet it is written that we shall strive again
And I shall bind you for a thousand years.

LUCIFER. Written where? In Heaven? But the fair
page of Heaven
Was ever marred on earth. The earth is mine
And all that therein is. The people of earth
Are mine—all, all! And I have made them gifts—
War! Pestilence! Famine! Doubt and desola-
tion!
Look how they dote on me!

[*He indicates the* CITIZENS, *who have been watching with concerted reactions of hope and fear.* MICHAEL *moves towards them.*

MICHAEL. People of earth
You have broken the wings of prayer, and, without
faith,
How can you dare aspire to the ear of God?

CITIZENS (*murmuring*). Blessed Saint Michael—hear us,
help us!

MICHAEL. Be of good courage!
God is forever merciful. He bade me
Come to your aid.
(*Holding out his bound hands.*) But I am bound by sin—
By your sin. Look! Turn from your sin towards
faith.
And loose my hands. There is work for me——

[*The* CITIZENS *make a timid concerted movement towards* MICHAEL, *but* LUCIFER *springs between them and* MICHAEL, *driving them back in huddled fear with a great sweep of his sword.*

LUCIFER. Do not dare !
Back to your darkness !

MICHAEL. Stand, you doubtful ones !
Take faith and stand firm, that you may loose my
bonds
And I may strike the darkness out from the light
Forever !

[*But the* CITIZENS, *menaced by* LUCIFER, *crouch in fear.*
LUCIFER *laughs.*

LUCIFER. Ah ! See how they heed you, Michael.
They love my pretty toys.

[LUCIFER, *contemptuous though watchful, draws back a little
towards* L., *leaving the stage to* MICHAEL.

CITIZENS. What shall we do ?
Alas ! what shall we do ? Where is redemption
For such as we are ?

MICHAEL. Redemption is never far beyond repentance,
For God is merciful to men and sparrows.
But not repentance only shall direct you
To mercy. There is more required of you :
Courage of each to take firm hold again
On faith and hope ; to face again the skull
Whose hollow eyes glare dread on Golgotha
And look beyond, to the calm gaze of God.

1ST CITIZEN. But we have courage.

2ND CITIZEN. We have proved our courage.

3RD CITIZEN. What generation of men has better proof ?

MICHAEL. The sons of men were never strange to courage
Of earthly sort, and you have borne yourselves
As men indeed, and paragons, in these days
When the earth trembles and faints in the empty
travail
Of a lesser Armageddon. You have given your sons
a song.
What you have done shall be loud in the song of earth
While ever a spark of earth remains ; till the tongue
and the brain and the heart

13

Of the last man shall fade. . . . But this is courage
Not unalloyed. There is dross in the gold, and the
   peril
And fire have not purged it all. I would give you
   courage
Where the red heart has made a crucible
For living and pure gold.

CITIZENS (*despairing*).   Oh ! What shall avail
Of courage of common folk, the men in the street ?

2ND CITIZEN. We are no lords and leaders of men who
   may do great things
Of good and ill——

3RD CITIZEN.   And blaze the illuminations
On history's parchment pages——

1ST CITIZEN. Even in travail we are the common men of
   the street ;
The common women of the hearth and home,
Having no great names——

MICHAEL (*gently*).   Was *His* so great a name—
Jesus the son of Joseph, carpenter
Of Nazareth—until He made it so ?

LUCIFER (*sneering*). His faith has left His church. His
   church is ruined.

MICHAEL (*sternly*). Were every stone from every stone
   o'erturned,
Yet would the prayers that hallow all this place,
The faith of those who built to the glory of God,
The songs of all who sang to the praise of God,
The cares of all who brought their cares to God
Through all the centuries, from dark age to dark age,
Preserve it whole and perfect in His eyes.

  [*To the* CITIZENS.
Listen ! Can you not hear their voices ;
Voices that sang, five centuries ago,
In a simple and perfect faith ?

[MICHAEL *has lifted his head and stands listening. Fade
in the music of a medieval chant, or, if preferred, unaccompanied*

*voices singing an old hymn or a psalm (perhaps " I will lift
up mine eyes unto the hills"), very softly for a moment, as if
over a great distance of time. The CITIZENS rise and group
together to one side of the lowest platform, the side opposite that
which the PILGRIMS will occupy, listening, interested, momentarily hopeful. Then the music grows louder and/or voices are
definitely heard. The PILGRIMS enter the building by the main
entrance, and move in procession, singing still if they are to
sing, through the audience and up to the lowest platform, where
they group opposite the CITIZENS. If desired, quite a large
procession may be formed, and they may carry a banner or two
for greater pictorial effect (but there should not be too many of
them for effective handling in the space available). If there
are only a few of them, they enter as a group and not as a procession. They do not see the CITIZENS, nor are they aware of
the ruin of the cathedral, because they are as yet in the past.
MICHAEL and LUCIFER are still invisible to them. MICHAEL
moves up to the highest platform and stands to R. of the altar.
LUCIFER remains well over to L. of the middle platform, watching with some uneasiness. The PILGRIMS remain in a group
on the lowest platform until they have finished their singing and
the following lines.*

1ST CITIZEN (*awed*). They do not see us. They do not
see the angels.

2ND CITIZEN. Yet we see them. What a marvel is this ?

3RD CITIZEN. They are here in the past—five hundred
years ago.

1ST PILGRIM (*a dignified old man, looking about him*). Well,
here we are, my friends, at the end of our pilgrimage,
and this is the cathedral.

2ND PILGRIM (*a plump and garrulous woman*). It is a fine
building indeed, and must have cost a pretty penny.
But no doubt there will be wondrous cures and miracles
done here. God and Saint Michael will bless these
walls, you may depend upon that !

3RD PILGRIM (*a young girl*). It is beautiful ! God and
His holy saints must surely love to dwell in such a house.

2ND PILGRIM (*her tongue not stilled by her surroundings, but her
heart good*). I wonder if my Thomas is even now cured

of the humours of his joints? 'Twas for that—for one thing—I came, though 'a will take a gallon of ale to's breakfast—for all I can say, and that's much—and I don't doubt his joints suffer from his habits. Ah me! the good Saint Michael will have hard work to cure Thomas.

LUCIFER (*mocking, to* MICHAEL). New work for you, Michael. Don't stand here idle. Speed you and cure Thomas. (*No one takes any notice of this.*)

2ND PILGRIM. And there's Gaffer Woodrow's mule. The Devil's in the beast. (LUCIFER *chuckles, but again no one takes any notice.*) Poor Gaffer says t' me ere I left: " Gossip Bounce," he says, " for the love of God, put up a prayer for the quieting o' my pestilent beast," he says, " 'tis more than mortal man may do, an' I be sorely kicked and sore withal."

3RD PILGRIM. But—isn't it strange to bring such a thing to God—a mule, I mean?

1ST PILGRIM. We may bring all our cares to God, whether our own ills, or the ills of the weather, the crops, the beasts. God understands. God made mules as well as men.

2ND PILGRIM. And 'tis very certain that, if I bring not the mule to God in my prayers, no one will get 'n anywhere else, for not one step will the creature move unless it sorts with his liking.

3RD PILGRIM. I came first to see the wonder of the cathedral, and I shall pray here my ordinary prayers.

2ND PILGRIM (*teasing*). For a good man, a home, and a pair o' children, I doubt not. That's ever a maid's prayer. (*Confidentially.*) Pray not for more than two little ones, my dear. They be generally given in greater abundance than we poor women can properly do wi'.

[*Sniggers from some of the other* PILGRIMS. *The* 3RD PILGRIM *is confused.*

1ST PILGRIM (*to* 2ND PILGRIM). Gossip Bounce, you're a good woman and a good neighbour, as all know. But your tongue's too long—and this is church.

2ND PILGRIM. And where more than in church should a body speak her mind, so be she speaks truth ?

1ST PILGRIM (*thoughtfully*). Ay, 'tis in the little things of our lives God should be, as well as the great. But let's to our prayers, not forgetting those who would have come with us but lacked the time or the money.

2ND PILGRIM. I've a-many to remember, s' many as Carrier when he do go to town. And they must travel in my poor head, for I'm no gentlewoman wi' the gifts o' writing, nor scholard t' read it.
[*She begins to count on her fingers in some agitation, muttering to herself. The other* PILGRIMS *move up to the steps before the altar and kneel in a line, while she is still feverishly trying to remember all for whom she has prayers to make.*

LUCIFER (*chuckling*). Look at the old gossip. I'll go and whisper a naughty thought into her ear.
[*He moves towards the* 2ND PILGRIM, *but* MICHAEL *moves swiftly between them.*

MICHAEL. Back, Lucifer ! She is on God's work.

LUCIFER (*falling back, sneering*). Then God chooses peculiar agents.

MICHAEL (*coldly*). That has always been a habit of His.
[*The* 2ND PILGRIM *realizes that she is standing alone, gasps, and darts up to the others, plumping down on her knees in a vacant place.*

1ST CITIZEN (*awed*). Can they not see the ruin of this place ?

3RD CITIZEN. They are in the past, I tell you.

2ND CITIZEN. They had faith.
They brought their ills, little and big, to God,
In the sure knowledge that God would hear them,
heal them.

CITIZENS. They knew that God would hear. They had never a doubt.

1ST CITIZEN. But we are oppressed, we are afflicted with a heavy burden,
Losing the consciousness of God——

2ND CITIZEN.   Yet keeping the knowledge of our sin.

1ST CITIZEN.   For we are sophisticated, no longer simple
    as they.
        The machine age, the progress of civilization——

3RD CITIZEN.   If we may call it progress——

1ST CITIZEN.   Have done this to us.

2ND CITIZEN.   And now there is none to help us,
    Who cannot help ourselves.

CITIZENS.   Who cannot help ourselves.

LUCIFER (*to the* CITIZENS, *easily*).   Do not be over-impressed
    by this peep-show of the past.   You can see a better
    show at the cinema, any week.   And don't be taken in
    by their apparent piety.   They were no better than you
    are.   The only difference is that you have stopped pre-
    tending to yourselves.   Only children pretend now.
        [MICHAEL *makes another appeal to the* CITIZENS.

MICHAEL. Do not mistake reality for pretence,
        Or, turning to the candle, leave the sun.
        Have you no hearts more to lift in worship and
            peril ?
        No eyes to see the sweeping wings of angels
        Ever about you ? nor any ears to hear
        The music of the stars chanting together
        And all the sons of God singing for joy ? . . .
        They sing yet as they sang on that one day
        When God the Architect laid in the keystone
        Of His great arch that spans the universe,
        Holding the spaces of the firmament,
        And said : " It is done, and it is very good ! "

LUCIFER (*laughing*).   Your theme is threadbare, Michael.
            They have forgot
        Such antique miracles as the Creation.
        They know that male and female were created,
        (They found that out for themselves) but 'tis no
            more
        Than theme for magazine tale and celluloid—
        They call it love.   If you'll be advised by me,

You'll tackle them with something up-to-date :
The miracle of the great four-engined bomber
(One of my choicest angels), or the atom
Unleashed, bringing my latest mode in death,
The poetry of complex mechanism,
Or the complexity of politics.
Stir up your ideas, Michael——

MICHAEL (*scornfully*).   Get you behind me !
You who teach fools to sneer, and light the cackle
Of the laughter of madmen after baubles. I,
With the help of God, shall yet prevail against you.

CITIZENS (*reviving a little*). Is it possible
That we have begun to see again the gleam of truth
Living beyond the greater glare of the lie ?

1ST CITIZEN. Is it possible
That these good people, out of their past, can show us
That faith lives, however fitfully ?

LUCIFER.   No !
That lantern has gone out.

MICHAEL.   There is a light in darkness,
However your minds as yet fall back from know-
    ledge,
For everything is possible to God.

[*The* PILGRIMS *rise from their knees.*

1ST PILGRIM. I will lift up mine eyes unto the hills,
From whence cometh my help.

PILGRIMS. My help cometh even from the Lord,
Who hath made Heaven and earth.

3RD CITIZEN. It is a beautiful thing to have a faith like
that.

2ND CITIZEN. To have it, too, for every moment of one's
workaday life.

1ST CITIZEN. With such a faith, we could rebuild the world.

LUCIFER (*angrily*). This has gone on long enough. (*To
the* CITIZENS.) I tell you these people are common clay,
weak as you are. They prattle like children who have

never seen reality. I will show you how much their faith is worth.

[*He moves swiftly upstage to the highest level, standing between the* PILGRIMS *and the altar.*
You can't have God without me. Behold !

(*The* PILGRIMS *see him, gasp, and shrink back in horror.*)

2ND PILGRIM. Why 'tis the Devil, for all a's in his Sunday best.

1ST PILGRIM. Lucifer ! Here at the very altar ?

3RD PILGRIM. Here among prayer and beauty built for God ?

PILGRIMS (*horrified*). Are our prayers lacking in strength ? . . .
　　If we cannot avoid the Devil,
　　How shall we reach God ?

LUCIFER (*terribly*). I am among you, you fools who think that your ills and ailments, your wars and the fears of hunger and death that are always upon you, shall be cured by a mere pilgrimage to a place made of wood and stones.

MICHAEL. A place hallowed by prayer.

LUCIFER (*to the* PILGRIMS). Look at the cross ! You think it strong and upright—but look again.

[LUCIFER *makes a sweeping gesture towards the cross. The* PILGRIMS *look and are dismayed.*

PILGRIMS (*horrified*). The cross has fallen ! Who has dared to overthrow the cross ?

1ST PILGRIM (*to* LUCIFER). You are the enemy ! You have done this !

LUCIFER. And God has not been able to prevent me. (*He makes gestures about and upward.*) Look ! . . .
　　See all the ruin—all !
　　Watch all your hopes tumbling about your ears
　　As these stones tumbled.

[*The* PILGRIMS, *huddled together, look about them fearfully.*

1ST PILGRIM.　　　　　　　　　We do not understand.

2ND PILGRIM. It is as though a thousand years and more
   Had passed over the place——

1ST PILGRIM. And it untended
   A thousand years, by hand or heart of man.

3RD PILGRIM. And for a thousand years devoid of prayer.

PILGRIMS. Oh, Michael ! Blessed Saint Michael ! How
is your church destroyed !

MICHAEL. God's Church is not destroyed until all faith
is dead. And nothing can destroy the prayers of those
who believe in prayer.

[*The* PILGRIMS *turn and see* MICHAEL. *They are amazed
and relieved, bowing themselves before him.*

PILGRIMS. Blessed Saint Michael ! Help us !

LUCIFER (*chuckling*). Look at his hands.

PILGRIMS (*horrified*). His hands are bound ! What has
bound his hands ?

LUCIFER (*indicating the* CITIZENS). They have helped me
to bind his hands.

[*The* PILGRIMS *see the* CITIZENS *and are again amazed,
making hesitant, fearful but curious movements downstage
towards them.*

2ND PILGRIM. What strange beings are these ? Are we
bewitched ?

3RD PILGRIM. See ! They are bowed in grief. Is their
grief like ours ?

1ST PILGRIM. Are they men like us—with their hope killed
Suddenly ?

3RD PILGRIM. And joy dead in a flash—like beauty.

MICHAEL. They are the men who shall build this church
again.

1ST PILGRIM (*doubting*). Yet—they have bound your
hands ?

MICHAEL. But you shall teach them
   That bound may be unbound.

PILGRIMS (*doubting*).　　　　　How shall we teach them
　　　What we ourselves—now—do not know ? If God
　　　Cannot protect His own church, how shall He
　　　succour us ?
　　　How may we help you ? How believe again
　　　In any good ?

MICHAEL (*warning*). Keep hold on faith.

2ND PILGRIM.　　　　Was it faith that brought us here ?
　　　Here, to a ruined church with evil abroad in it ?

3RD PILGRIM. And good—bound ?

　　　[*The* PILGRIMS, *filled with doubt and fear, are now in a
　　group to R. of the second platform. The* CITIZENS *are kneeling
　　to L. of the lowest platform.* LUCIFER *is upstage L. and*
　　MICHAEL *downstage R.*

LUCIFER (*pleasantly, to the* PILGRIMS, *indicating the* CITIZENS).
　　These are the men who live in your world five hundred
　　years after you. (*Laughing, again indicating the ruins.*)
　　You see how beautiful they have made the world.

1ST PILGRIM (*gravely, to* 1ST CITIZEN). Is this true ?

1ST CITIZEN (*sadly*). It is true.

2ND PILGRIM (*to* 2ND CITIZEN). We had our sins and our
　　wars and our troubles—ay, we're no more than poor
　　simple sinners, the best of us. But you've had five
　　hundred years to learn better than we.

2ND CITIZEN (*sadly*). Near two thousand years since
　　Calvary.

3RD PILGRIM (*wondering, to* 3RD CITIZEN). Yet you have
　　learned no better ?

3RD CITIZEN (*sadly*). We have learned no better. We have
　　learned only to make greater troubles and greater wars.

PILGRIMS (*sadly*). Then what hope for the world ?

CITIZENS (*sadly*). What hope for the world, indeed ?

MICHAEL. Hope goes always hand-in-hand with faith.

LUCIFER. But they have no faith. There is no faith.

　　　[*The* PILGRIMS *move sadly down to the lowest platform and
　　group themselves opposite the* CITIZENS, *kneeling and crouching*

in the same attitudes. MICHAEL *is sad.* LUCIFER *is triumphant.* MICHAEL *lifts his head, making a great effort.*

MICHAEL (*passionately*). Is it for this Christ hangs upon
the cross
Three hours—and twenty centuries? Is there no
flame
Can light again these dulled souls? *To hope by faith,*
To faith through beauty. Is there no power of beauty
Yet living on the earth? Is God's gift of the rose
Less lovely than of old? Are there no powers in
music?

[*A brief passage of music, very soft and distant, broken off*
after a few notes—a mere whisper of music as if to MICHAEL'S
imagination alone. The PILGRIMS *and* CITIZENS *do not hear*
it. LUCIFER *is sardonic. But* MICHAEL, *listening, is in-*
spired. He addresses the CITIZENS *more vigorously.*

Listen again!
God, making man in His own image, gave him
A little spark of godhead, so creating
Craftsman and craft alike, artist and vision
Meet for great works to the greater glory of God.
The living stone He gave, rich woods and metals,
Pigments, and all the ecstasy of sounds
In their innumerable variations
From the leaf's whisper to His loudest music
That sets the pattern of the dreadful fugue
Backing the tempest—thunder. These He gave,
And infinite variety of form;
Curved grass-leaf, cloudy galleon, the small wing
Of the ephemeral mayfly, and the grace
Of the sleek panther. He gave man eyes to see,
And a heart to burn, and hands to reach toward
beauty,
And a mind humbly to hold the vision of beauty,
Toward which—in truth—no man may look with-
out seeing
Some shadow of a mightier thing beyond
His present comprehension.

[*The* CITIZENS *have lifted their heads, catching something of*
MICHAEL'S *inspiration. They stand up.*

I WILL ARISE !

CITIZENS. We have known beauty,
 Fitfully glimpsed. Never abiding. Music——

LUCIFER (*sardonically*).   What ? Jazz ?

CITIZENS. Words bright and sharp as swords——

LUCIFER.   And sticky crooners'
 Treacle to catch unthinking flies, with their loves
  and doves
 And moons and Junes, where silly boy meets girl
 To make a pair of morons and breed more,
 More, ever more of morons, while the world rots.

CITIZENS. We have seen beauty in gulls' wings——

LUCIFER.   What of their beaks
 Curved to rend flesh and offal ?

CITIZENS.   We have seen
 The lovely filigree of silver branches
 Through a veil of mist——

LUCIFER.   And grumbled at the rain.

CITIZENS. And all the beauties of Nature——

LUCIFER (*enjoying himself*).   *All* of them.
 The toad, the ass, the warthog and the duck,
 God's jokes and misfits. And you have also known
 The blind, the maimed, the mad ; those who are
  blighted
 For the sins of their fathers before them, visited
 By a jealous God on several generations.
 Beauty ? (*Laughs contemptuously.*) Faugh !

CITIZENS.   Surpassing beauty of woman
 Made to conceive man in the shape of God.

LUCIFER (*mocking*). Woman ? Supreme ? Showing her
 thighs for hire
 In the front row of the chorus.
 (*Bowing ironically to* MICHAEL.) Your move, I think.
 Or will you own you are beaten, and give up
 This poor, half-damp, half-kindled human stuff
 To me, their master ? See Hell's paving-stones
 Of good intentions, bowing down their backs.
 I find them very funny, otherwise

I WILL ARISE !

I'd really rather give them back to God
And let Him sit eternally and watch
His greatest failure stewing in its juice.

[LUCIFER *is overcome with laughter.*

MICHAEL (*coldly*). You ever had one fault—you talk too
much.
Your argument is cheap and over-coloured.
I've always heard Hell is a gaudy place
Blunting the taste.

LUCIFER (*amused*).   Come down and see for yourself.
We'll give you special welcome, quite regardless
Of any expense——

MICHAEL (*impatiently*).   Enough ! You waste my time.

[LUCIFER *chuckles.* MICHAEL *moves upstage and stands in
thought, his head raised. He speaks as if to himself.*
To faith—through beauty. . . .. Beauty is manifest
In a myriad ways to man, however flawed
And short of Heaven's perfection. How shall I
show them ?

LUCIFER. You waste your own time.

MICHAEL.   Beauty with honesty,
With high devotion—and with a simple heart,
Of such is the Kingdom of Heaven.

[*Brief music, a simple medieval piece.* MICHAEL *looks R.
or downstage as on a sudden decision, beckoning with his bound
hands.*
Ah ! Come, my friend,
Come ! Tell them what you dreamed of in your
day
And what were the fruits of dream.

[*The* ARCHITECT *enters R. or through the audience. The
music stops as he speaks to the* CITIZENS.

ARCHITECT.   I dreamed in stone ;
In beauty of strong stone, pillar and arch
Springing from true foundation ; chancel and nave,
Triforium and clerestory ; the fretted wonder
Of windows all about the illumined saints

And angels in coloured glass.   And, above all,
The soaring benediction of the spire.

[*With a gesture which indicates that he still sees his cathedral
as standing.*

Look to what amplitude my dream was wrought
By God's good help.

[*He is the only one who does not see the ruin of the cathedral.*
MICHAEL *watches him with affection,* LUCIFER *sardonically.
The* CITIZENS *and* PILGRIMS *are despairing, in crouching
groups.*

LUCIFER. *What* do you see ?

ARCHITECT (*calmly, not looking at* LUCIFER). I see
What I have said.   And I should know, who made it.
Not a shoddy piece, nor a flawed stone.

LUCIFER. You fool !
Look now !

[LUCIFER *bounds before the* ARCHITECT, *passing his hand
before his eyes.   The* ARCHITECT *starts back, fearful, then
forgets* LUCIFER *as he sees the ruin of his work.   For a moment
he stands in silence, reacting to what he sees, himself broken.*

ARCHITECT. My lovely church—broken and burned !
Arch—pillar—tracery gone !

[MICHAEL *steps down to the side of the* ARCHITECT, *to
encourage him.*

MICHAEL. Five hundred years
And more, it stood.

ARCHITECT. It should have stayed a thousand.
Oh, what a work of devils is this !

MICHAEL. Of devils indeed !
But Hell yawns wide for devils. . . . Your cathedral
Is part already of eternal Heaven
Since men draw up to Heaven what lifts them there
In a divine reciprocation——

ARCHITECT (*too hurt to respond*). I——
Forgive me, sir.   I do not understand,
I am out of my proper time, and all o'erborne
With broken stones.   I pray your pardon, sir.

I know not which is Heaven and which is Hell,
Save that I see Hell round me.

MICHAEL. Yet your church
Stands full and perfect still in the eyes of God.
And men—do you inspire them—will complete
The earthly shape again.

[LUCIFER *laughs*.

ARCHITECT. I do not know.
It is a high thing you speak of, and my brain
Turns only on ruined work. I beg you give me
Leave to reflect awhile, to mourn awhile.

[*The* ARCHITECT, *his head bowed, goes to the L. side of the
stage and sits on a block of masonry. From time to time he
lifts his head to gaze sorrowfully at the ruin about him, then
bows his face again between his hands. The* CITIZENS *and*
PILGRIMS *sink deeper into despair.* MICHAEL *bows his head.*
LUCIFER *is triumphant.*

LUCIFER (*to* MICHAEL). So much for *that* trick. (*To the*
CITIZENS.)

Now *I* could show you tricks
Were I minded. I was ever a good showman.
We own the finest circus in the universe
And certainly the greatest show on earth !
Admission to the first performance free ;
To the second—but a payment of no value,
A thing of no account—your soul. (*Laughing.*)
What ? Beauty ?
And how should that inspire you ?
You see it at the pictures every week
(Some of you twice a week), full four times life-size
Close ups of lips, of legs, of glycerine tears
And false long eyelashes, from Hollywood.
And you are satiate with sugared beauty,
The only kind you know. How many of you
Have opened Shakespeare, since you sat at lessons
And read him, willynilly, bowdlerized ?
How many of you are really fond of Bach ?
Or love the paintings of Augustus John ?

Or dote on Epstein, when he isn't vulgar ?
Beauty ?   You need no beauty—not his kind.

[*He indicates* MICHAEL.

Cold churches—colder saints, all iced with faith
And stiffened up with virtue.   I can give you
Something brighter and warmer——

[*The* CITIZENS *are now at once repelled and fascinated by*
LUCIFER.

1ST CITIZEN. There is a doom upon us !

CITIZENS. We are doomed to hate ; doomed to leave that
we would have——

3RD CITIZEN. Or think we would have——

CITIZENS. And follow that we would not.

1ST CITIZEN.   The finest things
Pass all above our heads——

2ND CITIZEN.   We are doomed to snatch
Always the second-rate——

3RD CITIZEN.   Always the meretricious.
We seek the glitter of gold.

1ST CITIZEN.   There is no glitter in faith,
So we have let faith slip out of our minds, our souls.

3RD CITIZEN. Leaving emptiness.

2ND CITIZEN.   Into an empty place
The Devil always enters.

3RD CITIZEN.   Into a soul devoid of God
Another master comes.

1ST CITIZEN.   Yesterday and to-morrow
It is always the same.   The doom !

CITIZENS and PILGRIMS.   The doom upon us !
(*In passionate appeal.*)
Oh God ! Who made the fire and the metal to
forge in the fire,
And the world and the love and the homely things
to consume in the fire,
Have mercy upon us !

28

I WILL ARISE!

Oh Christ! Who on the splintered cross could
  bear the unbearable pain
Of one forsaken awhile even by God,
Have mercy upon us!
Christ, have mercy upon us!

MICHAEL (*lifting his head*).   *How* do you call on God
  And on His Son? From custom only and fear,
  As little children, waking in the dark,
  Call on their mothers? (*With a little more hope.*)
    Or do you cry in truth
  From the lingering hunger of a faith yet living
  And craving sustenance?

CITIZENS and PILGRIMS (*uninspired, merely fearful*). We cry
  for mercy.

MICHAEL (*disappointed, but persisting*).

But scarce knowing to Whom you make your cry,
God is a name to you, a power remote
And vague. You must reach further, and remember
That God sent down His Son to gather manhood
And *your* weakness and *your* every temptation,
That Christ, being man, might suffer as you do
And know your doubts and dangers; that, being
  man,

He might show all men all that man might be,
And, in that showing, forever make Himself
At once a perfect example of man, and mirror
Of God's Own likeness. (*Pause.*) Listen! Think
  on this:

Christ went alone into the great darkness
As very man, making the flesh of man
Strong to endure the pain; making His Spirit
Accept the utterest degradation,
And, through it all, in that waste land of doubt
He kept His faith alight. (*Pause.*) That is the test.
Not suffering endured only with courage,
But suffering lit with an unfaltering faith
In a living God, made real in the person of Christ.

29

CITIZENS and PILGRIMS (*still doubtful*).

> It is hard, the path you show us, and we are weak.
> If Christ would come again——

MICHAEL.   He may not come,

> For God, through Him, has given the world one chance
> The world has not yet taken. Even God
> May not again offer His Son to die
> For the sins of man.
> [*In sharp question.*

>   Do you cry indeed from the soul ?
> [*The* CITIZENS *and* PILGRIMS *bow their heads, not able to reply.*

LUCIFER.   They cry from naught more heavenly than fear.

> [*He leaves the* CITIZENS *and goes up to* MICHAEL, *tempting him.*

> Do not cling longer to a lost cause, Michael.
> Lost causes are uncomfortable things.
> My terms are generous for an armistice :
> You shall have rank and honour in my kingdom,
> And I—no more than what is mine already—
> The immortal part of man.

MICHAEL (*angrily*).   Do you dare tempt *me* ?

> You are enough to try the very patience
> Of an archangel. (*Calmer.*) But I will bear with you
> A little longer. I shall break your wings
> And bind you, in God's time.

LUCIFER (*drawing himself up, furious and terrible*).   You shall bind *me* ?

> Come, all you powers of Hell ! This is *our* day !

> [*Stormy music and thunder.* LUCIFER, *with a sweeping movement of anger, raises his sword and, with great (stylized) blows that clang on* MICHAEL'S *armour, drives him about the stage.* MICHAEL, *unable to defend himself because of his bound hands, falls back from* LUCIFER *and, wounded, sinks against a block of masonry to R. The* CITIZENS *and* PILGRIMS *react in concerted movements of horror, groaning. During the struggle the following lines are said, sharp and staccato with fear.*

I WILL ARISE !

1ST PILGRIM.   God has given the earth to ruin !

1ST CITIZEN.   God has sickened of our sins !

2ND PILGRIM.   We have no escape from hell !

2ND CITIZEN.   We have sinned and we must die !

3RD PILGRIM.   Prayer and faith are an illusion !

3RD CITIZEN.   Even the angels die with us !

[*The struggle and the music stop.*

ARCHITECT (*standing up*). Oh God ! I spared not blood
nor brain to build You a worthy house—but You let
Your enemies destroy it, and who shall build it again ?
Could You indeed be God, and not prevent this thing ?

MICHAEL (*wearily, leaning against the stone*). Oh God—is
there no spark of faith ? Is this the end of all Your
creation, and the end of man ? You are merciful, but
man has not deserved Your further mercy. (*Passionately.*) Father of all !—if there be ten still faithful—or
but two——

[MICHAEL *stops, exhausted.*

1ST CITIZEN (*despairing*). To what shall we look forward ?
　　Shall we look to the black ruin that once was
　　　　Heaven ?
　　To a desolation of angels' broken wings ?

CITIZENS and PILGRIMS. Shall we lift our eyes to the
　　　　empty and echoing hills ?
　　Shall we bury our great grief in the depths of the
　　　　sea ?
　　Shall we, like Job, consider if it were better
　　To curse God and die ?

MICHAEL (*lifting his head, with a great effort*). You shall
look again into your hearts. Perhaps there yet remains
a spark of faith to be kindled. Look now—swiftly—for
I am all but spent——

[*But the* CITIZENS, PILGRIMS *and* ARCHITECT *remain
despairing.* MICHAEL *sinks lower against the stone.* LUCIFER
moves down to address the CITIZENS *and* PILGRIMS.

31

I WILL ARISE !

LUCIFER (*mocking*). Faith? Faith in a scheme of things
that is no more than a wheel turning stupidly ever in
the same place, bringing ever the same sequence of
trials? Birth and pain and fear! Hunger and pain
and struggle! War and pain and death! Shall one
have faith in a wheel whose spokes are always pain?

CITIZENS. The daily round, the common task,
    Furnishing little but the weekly wages
    When one is very lucky.

1ST CITIZEN.   At best it is
    A rather dreary round, and then, too often,
    A terror of unemployment——

2ND CITIZEN.   Degradation
    Of the dole queue, of the dolorous dole——

3RD CITIZEN. Men standing with animal patience waiting
      a pittance
    Enough to keep the stomach faintly living——

2ND CITIZEN. But not the heart——

3RD CITIZEN.   Not the brain——

1ST CITIZEN.   Not, not the soul!

CITIZENS. And now in this day,
    War has o'erwhelmed us all in devastation,
    Fire, loss and ruin; pain to gild the days,
    The grey days of another common round.

PILGRIMS. As with you, so with us. But our lives were
      harder.
    For us there was no dole save charity,
    And that infrequent.

1ST PILGRIM.   Where a man fell out
    Of the race of life, he could lie and rot, for all
    Most men would care.

2ND PILGRIM.   And we, the poor, were crowded
    In filthy hovels. We tilled our little strips
    For a snatched living——

3RD PILGRIM.   In the flickering light
    Of our one poor candle holding at bay the dark,
    We could see more plain the shadows, but not see

What things of witchcraft hovered in the shadows,
Known and unknown, ready to pounce——

2ND PILGRIM. The darkness,
Brought things lurking stealthy about our walls,
The terror by night, the evil by day——

1ST PILGRIM. The scourges
Of the plague, the sweating sickness, the Black
Death.

3RD PILGRIM. Though we had taken to ourselves these
trials
With no thought from the ordinary——

PILGRIMS. Yet now
We stay to ask : " How can a living God
So grievously afflict us ? Can it be possible,
Where such hard life is, there is a God at all ? "

PILGRIMS and CITIZENS. Horror ! There is no God ! We
are cast away !

CITIZENS. We have become of all men most unhappy.

PILGRIMS. Not for a lost faith only.

CITIZENS. No. For we see
There never has been an object of our faith.

PILGRIMS. This is our doom. We have followed only a
marsh-light.

CITIZENS. And now we are in the clinging mire and the
dark,
For there is no God !

PILGRIMS. There is no God !

PILGRIMS and CITIZENS. And all
Is emptiness !

[*The* CITIZENS *and* PILGRIMS *bow themselves in despair.*
LUCIFER *addresses them, pleasantly.*

LUCIFER. My friends—ancient and modern. You have
something that I happen to want ; something of no use
whatever to you, in fact you're far better without it.
Because, like a rotten tooth, it's apt to wake up and
hurt you sometimes. You may ask why I want what is

of no use to you, but that's easily answered. I am a collector, and collectors, as you know, are hardly ever quite sane about the things they collect. I want your old souls, my friends. And I can pay a big price for them—pleasure, sensation, ease and self-indulgence. And freedom from want and fear, as another gentleman said quite recently. Walk up, now, and sign on the dotted line. I'm a strict keeper of bargains.

[LUCIFER *takes a quill and a scroll from his dress, moves up to the altar and sits on it, waiting for his customers.*

1ST CITIZEN. We have come down, far down, through the sunless valley
To the place where hope sickens. Nevermore
Shall glad sound, or song of bird, or the voices of youth in laughter
Quicken our souls——

3RD PILGRIM. Or a new-springing note
Cleave through the veils of silence evermore
Clinging——

2ND CITIZEN. Clinging——

1ST PILGRIM. I mpenetrable——

3RD CITIZEN. Forbidding joy.

1ST CITIZEN. We have come down, far down, through the long valley
To a place of ultimate silence. Even pain
Is dulled now——

1ST PILGRIM. No more wounding. No more struggling and striving
In the clawed grip——

2ND CITIZEN. And what celestial gain
Ever has been for the writhing soul in the dark of pain ?

3RD PILGRIM. What is the use of it all ? What has ever been
The use of it all ?

3RD CITIZEN. We have been told that man is ennobled by suffering.
Have they suffered who told us ?

2ND PILGRIM. Do they offer
No more than a pretty dish of wishful thinking ?

PILGRIMS and CITIZENS. No more than that ?
Our souls are dead, dead as leaves that, lingering,
cling to the winter branch ;
Cling in despair, not hope, and, in their clinging,
Know they never shall know the sap springing.
Never again. Never know
Aught of burgeoning hope. And nevermore
Know anything of joy.
[*Brief pause, then, in dreary, matter-of-fact voices :*
Let us make the best bargain we are able to make.

MICHAEL (*another great effort*). No !

[*The* CITIZENS *and* PILGRIMS *take no notice of* MICHAEL,
but begin to make a tentative, concerted movement towards
LUCIFER, *as if about to offer their souls to him.* MICHAEL
weakly and vainly struggles with his bonds, crying out in agony.
Oh God ! Help us !

[*Faint, sweet music, perhaps an "Ave Maria."* MICHAEL
revives somewhat and looks up. The CITIZENS, PILGRIMS *and*
ARCHITECT *lift their heads in sudden new hope.* LUCIFER,
*angry and uneasy, shrinks back towards L. The music swells
up. There is a tense pause, as of breathless waiting. The*
YOUNG WOMAN *and* YOUNG MAN *enter, either R. or through
the audience, as ordinary visitors to the ruins. They stand
looking quietly about them for a moment, not seeing the other
characters, all of whom are intent on them. They see only the
ruined cathedral. The music fades out. They speak quite
simply, a little awed by their surroundings at first.*

YOUNG WOMAN. This is the cathedral. I knew it before
the war. I'm afraid I didn't appreciate it properly
then, but I've wanted to come back to it—now.

YOUNG MAN. So have I. Before the war I didn't think
much about things—religion and all that, I mean. But
now—well, all the pain and the courage and the waste
and the glory have made me think.

YOUNG WOMAN. Yes—a whole lot of us have come to
realize that we aren't put into the world just to chase

after what we used to call a good time. (*With a rueful little laugh.*) And not so good, either.

YOUNG MAN. Not so good—what we thought was happiness. We're meant to be happy, but we don't properly know what happiness is, or how to get it.

YOUNG WOMAN. We're learning. (*She indicates the ruins with a wide gesture.*) All this won't fail of its purpose.

YOUNG MAN (*thoughtfully*). When you look at it, what do you think of ?

YOUNG WOMAN. I think—— (*She hesitates a moment, then adds, impulsively :*) I think of Christ on His cross. I think of God Who deliberately took on a mass of troubles so that He could show us the way out of them. Yes— I think of Christ showing us what God is like and what man may rise to. (*Pause.*) You know, once one begins to think, one can't let go of these things. There's something—as though Someone is helping. . . .

YOUNG MAN (*eagerly*). Helping towards a vital belief—an active and everyday belief—that we've got the job of learning to stand properly upright, and of helping others to stand.

YOUNG WOMAN (*eagerly*). An everyday belief—God on weekdays. That's it ! (*Puzzled.*) Yet there's nothing so new in that ; nothing to shake the world.

YOUNG MAN. There's nothing new in it—but it could shake the world. You know, I've felt I had to make this—this pilgrimage, as soon as I could.

YOUNG WOMAN. That's just what I've felt about it—like the pilgrims of the Middle Ages. (*Pause, then, awed again :*) Do you feel that this cathedral inspires one now, even more than when it was whole and beautiful ?

YOUNG MAN (*awed*). Yes. As if these broken arches lift one to a truer sight of what are the great things, the good things. (*With growing confidence.*) I can see this : in the rebuilding of this cathedral, men will be rebuilding their own faith. (*On a sudden realization.*) Our coming here is an act of faith.

YOUNG WOMAN. An act of faith. (*Inspired.*) I believe
in the power and the love and the goodness of God.
I believe in the redemption of man through the sacrifice
and the example of Christ.

[*Brief pause. LUCIFER, thinking he had better do something
about this, goes to them.*

LUCIFER (*easily*). Don't talk a lot of sentimental nonsense,
my dear young people. You know very well that faith
is a delusion. And as for redemption——

[*He laughs, but his laugh quickly gives places to uneasiness.
They do not even know he is there.*

YOUNG MAN. Light after darkness ! And a perfection
building up through the ruin that man has made of the
world.

YOUNG WOMAN. A new world, where men can live together without strife and hatred—where I can bring up
children without envy and without fear.

YOUNG MAN (*taking her hands*). A world for all men—and
for us—without envy and without fear.

LUCIFER (*sourly*). And how many times in the world's
history, do you suppose, have silly young people like
you said silly young things like that ? It's only because
you're in love with each other—for what that's worth !

[*He walks round them. They still do not know he is there.
But the YOUNG WOMAN suddenly lifts her head and looks
towards MICHAEL, though without seeing him.*

YOUNG WOMAN (*awed*). There *is* something good here.
Not only the inspiration of this place, but something
more.

YOUNG MAN. I feel it, too. More even than the prayers
of ages that have soaked into the stone. There are so
many things we can't see—

YOUNG WOMAN (*confidently*). But we believe.

YOUNG MAN. Yes. We believe.

[*They look at each other for a moment, then go up to the altar
and kneel before it, still hand-in-hand. Music, soft and
distant, inspiring. The bonds slip from MICHAEL's hands.*

He straightens himself, spreading his hands at first a little from his sides, then gradually wider and higher with a suggestion of spreading wings. LUCIFER *watches him, afraid.*

MICHAEL (*at his full height, strong and confident*). Blessed are the pure in heart, for they shall see God.

[MICHAEL *draws his sword, taking it by the blade and holding it up before him like a cross. The music grows louder.* MICHAEL *cries in a ringing voice :*
In the Name of God, I drive all evil from His holy place !

[LUCIFER *shrinks away from* MICHAEL, *crouching, holding his left hand before his eyes as though to shut out the glory of* MICHAEL, *who advances on him, step by step, holding up the sword. The music changes to peals of thunder. Alternatively,* MICHAEL *drives* LUCIFER *off with sweeping, stylized blows of his sword,* LUCIFER *giving a great cry at each blow.* LUCIFER *backs away to L., his arms raised to shield his head, finally turning and plunging off L. amid a loud and then diminishing roll of thunder. The music has stopped. The* CITIZENS, PILGRIMS *and* ARCHITECT *watch tensely, reviving. The* YOUNG WOMAN *and* YOUNG MAN, *praying, taking no notice of the conflict. After* LUCIFER *is driven off,* MICHAEL *moves to upstage R. on the highest platform. The* ARCHITECT *joins the* PILGRIMS. *The* PILGRIMS *and* CITIZENS *regroup into two oblique lines, forming a sort of triangle without a base, the apex of which is just below the steps of the altar. Each individual looks towards the altar, with arms stretched towards the fallen cross.*

PILGRIMS and CITIZENS. Courage is new in our veins and our eyes are lifted
Towards the ultimate beauty. We tread the path
Of the high fulfilment of God's purpose for man :
That he should stand and look upward, not crawl on the earth.
We stand together in brotherhood. Naught shall affright us hereafter.

1ST CITIZEN and 1ST PILGRIM. Not the fear and the knowledge of sin and the heart that must ache in frustration——

2ND CITIZEN and 2ND PILGRIM. Not the soul that must
ever repent of its clinging portion of earth——

3RD CITIZEN and 3RD PILGRIM. Not the black wings of
the angel of death and the darkness to come——

PILGRIMS and CITIZENS. None of these things !
None of these things shall have power any more to
stay us,
For doubt, doubt is dead !

1ST PILGRIM. I have seen great good arising out of evil
Like a saint's prayers in the darkness.

1ST CITIZEN. And I have seen
Men's hearts and their courage renewed, and a
power of wings
Of legions of angels about us——

2ND PILGRIM. Lifting us up ;
Lifting our hearts and our eyes, that we crawl on
the earth no more.

2ND CITIZEN. I see that truth is immortal, goodness
eternal.
For God shall prevail in the end, and goodness and
truth are nourished
By the very hand of God.

3RD PILGRIM. I see a flower,
New-opened, blooming immaculate, on a dunghill,
The flower of faith——

3RD CITIZEN. And, after the flower, a star
Serene in the stormy heavens—the star of the
promise of God.

[*The* PILGRIMS *and* CITIZENS *move up in two lines towards
the fallen cross. The* YOUNG WOMAN *and* YOUNG MAN *rise
from their knees, turn, and move* **down** *to the lower level.*

PILGRIMS, CITIZENS and ARCHITECT. We will arise !
We accept the star and the struggle ;
We affirm the faith and the purpose ;
We take the pain with the joy ; the gain with the loss
Indivisibly knit. We accept the Christ and the
cross.

I WILL ARISE !

[*The* ARCHITECT *and* 1ST PILGRIM *and* CITIZEN *raise the cross and set it erect. They move away to their previous positions. The* ARCHITECT *stands just behind and slightly higher.* MICHAEL *moves to before the cross on the highest level, holding up his sword so that its hilt makes another cross. All are facing downstage towards the audience, with the* PILGRIMS *and* CITIZENS *grouped to either side.*

[*All, together with the audience, sing the " Te Deum " to an inspiring chant, or hymn* 431 *A. & M. (" Disposer supreme.")*

[*The players go off, singing, during the closing verses of the chant or hymn, in the following order :* YOUNG WOMAN *and* YOUNG MAN, CITIZENS, PILGRIMS, ARCHITECT.

[MICHAEL, *alone on the stage, speaks the following Epilogue :*

MICHAEL.   Here we end our mystery
        And, though all unworthily
        We have striven here to raise
        Your hearts and ours to God in praise,
        May our labours in this place
        Find acceptance of His grace,
        That His blessing now may fall
        On our work and on us all.

[MICHAEL *goes off, during a black-out if the performance is by artificial light.*

[*Concluding music, of a triumphal nature.*

T. B. MORRIS

Spanish Rhapsody

A Play in One Act

LONDON
FREDERICK MULLER LTD.
29 Great James Street, W.C.1

FIRST PUBLISHED BY FREDERICK MULLER, LTD.
IN 1948
PRINTED IN GREAT BRITAIN BY WYMAN & SONS LTD.
LONDON, READING AND FAKENHAM

Spanish Rhapsody was first presented by the Warwick Road Church Players, of Coventry, at the Little Theatre, on 22nd November, 1945, with the following cast :

Miguel Cardura	RONALD CHAYTOR
Alvara Rodriguez	PETER HUGHES
Baldomero Castro	RALPH HAINES
First Republican Soldier ..	FREDERICK GODDARD
Second Republican Soldier ..	KEITH WHETSTONE
Padre Don Fernando Diez ..	JOHN GREEN
Sancha León	ETHEL NELSON
Carmencita Monardes	CHRISTINE HARRIS
La Borrachera	DOROTHY BYRON
Doña Consuelo de Queveda ..	DOROTHY HOLLOWAY
Doña Teresa Jiminez	PAULINE ANSELL
Soledad Vallina	BERYL HARRIS
First Rebel Soldier	DEREK HANDS
Second Rebel Soldier	ALAN BERRY
Colonel Philip Adaja	SAMUEL LOXHAM

The play produced by ALBERT WHETSTONE.

TO
ANN AND ALBERT WHETSTONE

THE CHARACTERS

MIGUEL CARDURA, *local Commandante of Republican forces.*

ALVARO RODRIGUEZ, *his lieutenant.*

BALDOMERO CASTRO, *an innkeeper.*

FIRST REPUBLICAN SOLDIER*.

SECOND REPUBLICAN SOLDIER*.

PADRE DON FERNANDO DIEZ, *the village priest.*

SANCHA LEÓN, *an anarchist.*

CARMENCITA MONARDES, *a young girl* } *villagers.*

LA BORRACHERA, *an old woman*

DOÑA CONSUELO DE QUEVEDA, *a young aristocrat.*

DOÑA TERESA JIMINEZ, *her duenna.*

SOLEDAD VALLINA, *a young student.*

FIRST REBEL SOLDIER*

SECOND REBEL SOLDIER* } *of Franco's army.*

COLONEL PHILIP ADAJA

Other Villagers and Soldiers of both armies (*optional.*)

---

* The parts of the Two Soldiers may be doubled. As Republican soldiers they may wear their own clothes or blue overalls. As Rebel soldiers they should be in uniform (khaki drill with short-sleeved shirts open at the throat, no coats, peaked caps) and be much smarter. Colonel Adaja may also be without a coat if desired, with his sleeves short or rolled up, though his appearance must be smart.

THE SCENE

The street of a mountain village in Castile, somewhere south of Toledo, during the Spanish Civil War. A morning of September, 1936.

The scene may be simply or elaborately mounted. Following is a suggestion for a combination of cyclorama or backcloth with a curtain set.

The curtains backstage R. are drawn down straight and weighted at the foot to suggest a high wall, as of an old watch-tower. High on this may be a heavily barred window. Lower down is a large, vividly-coloured, but somewhat torn and weathered poster, preferably showing a matador and bull in action in addition to some or all of the following lettering, but otherwise done somewhat in the manner of an English circus poster.

(The dotted lines represent smaller lines which would not be visible at distance of audience. The names may be omitted if desired.)

Pascua, 1936
Atracción Grande !
CORRIDA DE TOROS

. . . .

TOLEDO

. . . .

DOMINGO ORTEGA
LALANDA
ARMILLITA

. . . .

DOMINGUIN DE TOLEDO

. . . .

(Easter, 1936, the poster an old one, as there would have been no recent bull-fighting.)

(These are the names of toreros who have fought at Toledo around this time.)
(Ex-torero turned impresario.)

47

The above poster is not essential, but will add colour and atmosphere to the set, and make the curtain " wall " more effective. Backstage L. the curtains are draped obliquely and gathered up to suggest rocks. On what is apparently a piece of the flat face of a rock (card or thick paper of same colour as curtains) is scrawled large in chalk VIVA FRANCO. The rest of the back of the stage is taken up by a large expanse of sunlit sky with a ground strip representing distant mountains. A broken wooden railing runs across the back of the stage, which is imagined as the edge of a precipice. Downstage R. another straight and weighted curtain forms a masking wall, and this will be improved by one of the wrought-iron balconies characteristic of Spanish houses (a silhouette of the end of this, cut in card or plywood, will suffice). Downstage L. is an inn sign, with large letters PARADOR DE LA ROSA, and beneath in smaller letters the proprietor's name, BALDOMERO CASTRO. This sign is fixed so that it projects on to the stage and suggests that the entrance to the inn is downstage L. This suggestion may be emphasized by clipped trees in tubs or flowering plants (such as geraniums) in large pots. A largish tree might mask the entrance downstage L. There may be smaller notices, such as advertisements for wines and lemonade (*limonada*), cigarettes and tobacco (*cigarrillos*, *tabaco*), etc., under imaginary trade names, as desired. Downstage L. there are one or two small outdoor tables, with chairs and/or benches. One or two of these are overturned, with any other possible indications that there has been recent fighting. (In a more elaborate set the walls themselves may show damage from shells.) If possible, the back portion of the stage should be a path raised by irregular steps above the level of the rest, to give a higher level immediately below the railing, the path itself rising from L. to R., where, at its highest point, it goes off behind the tower. It may be convenient to have the railing broken at this point so that it may be used for entrances and exits in the action to do with the cliff. Entrances at convenient points to R. and L., in addition to the above and the inn entrance.

(NOTE.—Particulars of records for warfare effects will be

found in the *Catalogue of Mood Music*, issued by the Central Record Information Bureau, " His Master's Voice," 363, Oxford Street, W.1.* In the event of uncertainty as to the pronunciation of such Spanish names as occur in the text, it will be advisable to consult someone who knows the language.)

* There is also much valuable information on the production of such effects in *Noises Off*, by Frank Napier (Frederick Muller, Ltd.)

SPANISH RHAPSODY

As the Curtain rises, MIGUEL CARDURA, *a young poet fighting for the Government forces, is sitting on a box somewhere upstage C. He wears an open-necked and short-sleeved shirt, a belt with a pistol in a holster, and breeches, shorts or trousers, as desired. He is tired and battle-stained, with a bandage round his head. Field-glasses are slung over his shoulder. At his left stands* ALVARO RODRIGUEZ, *an ex-matador, dark and flamboyantly handsome, also in some compromise between uniform and everyday clothes, but more showy in appearance than* CARDURA. RODRIGUEZ *also wears a pistol. The two men are very different,* CARDURA *an idealist, and* RODRIGUEZ *an opportunist and swaggerer. Downstage towards R., facing obliquely up to them, is* BALDOMERO CASTRO, *a plump and prosperous, oily, middle-aged innkeeper, dressed in a good suit of loud pattern. He is standing between* TWO REPUBLICAN SOLDIERS, *who have rifles but no uniforms (unless they wear the blue overalls worn by some of the Government forces). They are ragged, slouching, undisciplined, and have the cheeky independence of Gypsies. Somewhere towards C.L. is* PADRE DON FERNANDO DIEZ, *the village priest, a good old man, capable, on the one hand, of expressing the authority of the Church, and, on the other, of a rough humour suited to the villagers. He wears a cassock and crucifix. Backstage R., at the highest point of the path, is* SANCHA LEÓN, *a gaunt and forbidding, middle-aged woman with a knife thrust through the belt of her dark dress. Downstage L., leaning against one of the tables, is* CARMENCITA MONARDES, *a young girl in a bright but simple dress. She is afraid, but fascinated by what is going on. Other untidy* GOVERNMENT SOLDIERS, *together with* VILLAGERS *and* CHILDREN, *may be used as desired to build up groups to R. and L. All are tense, and* CASTRO *is increasingly fearful, his eyes shifting from* CARDURA *to* RODRIGUEZ *and back, his tongue licking over his lips, his hands spread ready for gestures which he is too fearful to make.*

51

CARDURA (*curtly*). You are Baldomero Castro, innkeeper ?

CASTRO. Yes, señor commandante.

CARDURA. What have you to say for yourself?

CASTRO (*an abrupt, broken-off gesture*). Señors—I swear by the Virgin, I——

RODRIGUEZ (*interrupting harshly*). We don't believe in virgins.

CASTRO. I am a good son of the revolution——

CARDURA. Yes—of Franco's revolution. You are known to have helped his rebels.

LEÓN. That's true. When the accursed swine came through from Trujillo yesterday with their blackamoors, you entertained their officers. I saw it. (*She laughs bitterly.*) You didn't think they'd be driven out so quickly.

CASTRO. What else could a man do ? (*His voice rising in fear.*) Mother of God ! what else ? I gave them a little wine—as little as possible—otherwise the dogs would have taken it all. But I've more wine—better wine—hidden—for patriots——

[LA BORRACHERA *enters downstage L. She is a wickedly humorous old woman, poorly dressed and dirty, who has well earned her nickname* (*drinking-bout*). *She carries a bottle of wine.*

LA BORRACHERA (*hearing the last line, cackling*). But not very well hidden—not well enough hidden, friend. You can't deceive La Borrachera. (*She flops on to one of the chairs and drinks noisily from the bottle.*)

CARDURA (*to* LA BORRACHERA). You heard my orders about looting——

LA BORRACHERA (*amused*). Looting, comrade ? Who'd think of it ? I'm a poor old woman—with no good saints to preserve me any more——

PADRE (*turning*). Now now——

LA BORRACHERA (*waving to the* PADRE *in friendly, impudent fashion*). —and I'm enjoying for the first time the

52

hospitality of the excellent Señor Don Baldormero Castro—(*spitting*)—may he burn in hell after you've shot him.

[*She laughs.* CASTRO *reacts fearfully, glancing wildly about him and taking a quick step back. Instantly the* SOLDIERS *menace him with their rifles.*

RODRIGUEZ. Take the fat swine away and shoot him. It's not only the wine. He's been giving information to the rebels——

CARDURA (*sternly*). Quiet, Rodriguez! I shoot no one without cause. Are we to copy Franco's pack of assassins?

LEÓN. Franco started murder! Give them blood for blood! Live, anarchy!

CARDURA (*rising, speaking with authority*). Enough of anarchy! We are patriots fighting for the established government of Spain. Live the Republic!

LA BORRACHERA.
CARMENCITA.
SOLDIERS. }Live, the Republic!
ANY SUPERS.

LEÓN. Live, anarchy!

[*During the following,* LA BORRACHERA *rises unsteadily and goes to the rock backstage, staring with suspicion at* VIVA FRANCO. *She spits on the word* FRANCO *and begins to rub it out.*

CARDURA. I am a poet. But I am also a Spaniard, and so I have thrown down the pen to fight for Spain. Remember that we are fighting on the side of our Republican government—a government pledged to improve the lot of the working people. This Franco and his reactionary friends would throw down liberty and democracy; they would exalt the rich against the poor; they would do to us what Mussolini and Hitler have done to the people of Italy and Germany. And they are fighting us with German and Italian troops and arms and money——

ALL (*except the* PADRE *and* CASTRO). Death to Franco !

CASTRO (*nervously, after the others*). D-death to Franco—and all rebels——

RODRIGUEZ. You won't save your miserable life that way.

CASTRO (*fearfully, to* CARDURA). Señor commandante—for the love of God——

RODRIGUEZ (*interrupting*). God isn't fashionable any more.

PADRE. My children ! Be careful of your words and deeds. God is not mocked—and blood demands more blood.

CARDURA (*gesturing all to silence*). You must learn this : our cause is high, and we must fight it with clean hands.

LA BORRACHERA (*cackling*). He who throws out offal can't avoid a stink. Who's got a piece of chalk !

RODRIGUEZ. What's the good of chalk to you, you illiterate old hag ?

LA BORRACHERA. Aha ! I am partly educated, friend. I can write two words.

[*The* 1ST REPUBLICAN SOLDIER *chuckles and throws her a piece of chalk. She blows him a derisive kiss and takes it up.*

1ST REPUBLICAN SOLDIER. I want it back. It is my pleasure to express myself rudely on railway bridges.

LA BORRACHERA. Thanks, comrade ! (*Cackling.*) I'll re-pay the favour—when it's dark.

[*The* SOLDIERS, RODRIGUEZ *and* LEÓN *laugh derisively.* LA BORRACHERA *goes back to the rock, and for the next few moments is painfully scrawling in large letters* LA REPUBLICA *in place of the deleted* FRANCO.

CARDURA. Now listen to me. The world's eyes are on us. The thinking men of Europe, America and Russia are with us. Our deeds must speak for the greatness of our cause.

RODRIGUEZ. Enough of words, then ! Let deeds speak ! We've wasted time on this innkeeper. There are others, too——

[*He glances at the* PADRE.

CARMENCITA. No, no!

PADRE (*calmly*). My son, I desire nothing for myself—least of all my life in these unhappy days. But I am of some little use——

RODRIGUEZ. Preaching your superstition——

PADRE (*sternly*). And how long have you thought it superstition? In your heart you still do not, Alvaro Rodriguez. I know you. (*He faces* RODRIGUEZ *with authority, so that* RODRIGUEZ *shrinks away from him for a moment.*) But I was speaking of material service. I've a little medical knowledge, and I use it without regard for side or faith or lack of it.

CARDURA. That's true enough, Father. We've no use for your Church. Religion and riches have always gone together——

PADRE (*almost humorously*). Indeed, my son, you can hardly accuse me of riches. I earn even less than a poet.

CARDURA (*a flicker of humour*). Impossible. (*Serious again.*) But you are brave and well-meaning. You are safe from us. (*Grimly.*) Only don't let your fine Christian General Franco hear that you patch up loyalists, or he'll have something to say to you.

LEÓN (*sardonically*). Ay! He'll say it with a bullet, and then blame the dirty anarchists and bolsheviks.

PADRE (*to* CARDURA). I came here to speak of this man. [*He indicates* CASTRO, *who lifts his head in sudden hope.*

CARDURA. Well?

PADRE. From what you have said, I feel you will hear me. Remember that man can only take life, not restore it.

CARDURA. I try to remember that. (*Bitterly.*) Franco's men shot my father and my brothers in Burgos—in cold blood. (*Pause.*) But I try to behave reasonably—if there can be reason where Spaniard fights Spaniard. (*Wearily, to the* SOLDIERS.) Take this fellow away and lock him up.

RODRIGUEZ. No !

LEÓN. Have you lost your senses ?

LA BORRACHERA. That's not wise, my pretty officer. A dead man gives no trouble.

PADRE (*to* CARDURA). Thank you, my son. (*He raises his hand in a friendly gesture.*) We need—mercy. God forgive us all.

[*The* PADRE *goes off* R.

CASTRO (*dropping on his knees before* CARDURA). Señor commandante—comrade—a thousand thanks——

[DOÑA CONSUELO DE QUEVEDA, *a lovely young aristocrat, well-dressed and in distinct contrast with the others, enters* L. *She is followed by* DOÑA TERESA JIMINEZ, *her duenna, a stiff but frightened lady of middle age. The others turn to look at* CONSUELO, *who is aware of her dangerous position, but confident of both power and beauty and faces them with a scornful courage.*

LEÓN. Aha ! Another throat to cut——

LA BORRACHERA (*who has returned to her drinking, cackling*). Pretty lady, pretty lady—come and be killed. (*Thoughtfully.*) There are many good patriots who could do with her finery. (*Looks at her own clothes.*)

CARDURA (*to the* SOLDIERS, *indicating* CASTRO). There is a cell at the police station. Shut him in that. I'll see to him later.

1ST REPUBLICAN SOLDIER (*airily*). Very well, señor comrade. But, if one may express an opinion——

2ND REPUBLICAN SOLDIER (*quite good-naturedly, to* CARDURA). You're a fool, señor comrade.

1ST REPUBLICAN SOLDIER. You take the words from my mouth, friend.

CARDURA (*angrily*). Be off with you !

2ND REPUBLICAN SOLDIER. At once, señor, at once. But we pause to remind you that, in a democratic state, every man is permitted to say what he thinks. (*To* CASTRO.) Come on, you overblown wine-skin.

[*Good-natured, as they would still have been if they were going to shoot* CASTRO, *they prod him off R. with their rifles. Any* SUPERS *follow them,*

CARDURA (*grimly, as they go*). You are responsible for him, remember. No accidents. There are too many atrocity stories about——

[*Meanwhile* RODRIGUEZ *has been giving interested glances at* CONSUELO *and swaggering a little under her not unappreciative gaze. He takes the opportunity of showing himself off to her.*

RODRIGUEZ (*to* CARDURA). I say you'll regret it. When I am in the bull-ring, I may appear foolhardy—I may kneel to receive the charge, the horns half an inch from my body—I may swing away and turn my back on him—ah, they cry, what daring ! (*He glances at* CONSUELO, *then begins to gesture.*) But there is a difference between bravery and foolhardiness. I know I have him—quickly I fix his eyes again. And when I take the sword for the kill—— (*He stands as if profiled to an imaginary bull on his left, his stomach sucked in, his body balanced lightly, his right arm stiffly across him at chin level, as though sighting along a sword held in a straight line with his arm*)—the precise moment—a hairsbreadth of error and the fight is bungled. But no——(*He makes an imaginary thrust to the left which he follows for a few steps as though passing along the bull's side, then jumps out of his pose*)—the stroke is true—the timing perfect—— (*He stands as if receiving the applause of an audience, then bows to* CONSUELO *and turns on* CARDURA *again.*) But you take your eyes from the bull too long—you ignore the danger of this innkeeper.

CONSUELO (*mischievously*). Bravo, matador !

LA BORRACHERA (*sardonically, dumping her bottle, now empty, at* RODRIGUEZ' *feet.*) It's empty—and that's all you deserve. A fine torero ! You've never so much as got an ear of a bull. Didn't the crowd hiss you out of the ring at Toledo ? You—bah ! (*Spits.*) You're no better than a prentice picador.

RODRIGUEZ (*furiously*). You damned old hag!

[*He darts at her, but she evades him and scuttles off L.,
cackling. Following her, he comes face to face with* CONSUELO,
*who is half-mocking, half-admiring. He tries to recover his
dignity by frightening her.*

And what do you want here, aristocrat? (*To* CARMEN-
CITA.) Bring some wine, girl.

[CARMENCITA *goes off downstage L.* RODRIGUEZ *turns
again to* CONSUELO.

Don't you know we've driven away your friends?

CONSUELO (*calmly*). For the moment. But never mind
that. They'll return when it suits them. In the mean-
time, I've come to see if there's a drop of decent olive
oil in the place—as no one else can do it for me——

TERESA (*nervously*). Señorita——

CONSUELO (*gesturing her to silence*). All I have is rancid—
faugh!

LEÓN. And why not? What's good enough for the poor
is good enough for you—and too good. Your friends
made this war.

CONSUELO. I am the Doña Consuelo de Queveda——

LEÓN (*mimicking her*). And I am the Doña Sancha
León—— (*Harshly*.) Fresh oil! Perdition—listen to
her! We have to use ours again and again, until our
cooking stinks like a herd of goats.

CONSUELO (*to* CARDURA). You are in command here—for
the moment?

CARDURA. I am in command here.

CONSUELO. Then I, a lady, make a reasonable request——

CARDURA. There is no fresh oil, señorita. And, if there
were, there are wounded men who need the best we
can give them.

CONSUELO. Wounded communists—rabble——

CARDURA. Take care. (*Thoughtfully*.) A year ago I
might have written sonnets to your eyes, but there's no
time, now, for pretty things like you.

CONSUELO (*with a lazy indifference*). Sonnets! My brothers would have horse-whipped you for insolence.

CARDURA (*harshly*). I said—take care!

RODRIGUEZ (*to* CONSUELO). No time, he says, for pretty things like you. He takes himself too seriously, this poet. Now I, Alvaro Rodriguez, can always find time for a lady young enough—and beautiful enough. (*Bowing.*) If I had my guitar——

LEÓN. There'd be a fine caterwauling, I've no doubt.

[RODRIGUEZ *tries haughtily to ignore this.* CARMENCITA *enters downstage L. with two bottles of wine and six glasses on a tray. She is going to* CARDURA, *but* RODRIGUEZ *stops her and takes a bottle and two glasses.*

RODRIGUEZ. As I have not, here is wine, señorita. You will drink with me.

CONSUELO. I will not drink with you.

RODRIGUEZ (*masterful*). You will do as you are told.

[*He goes to the nearest table and pours wine into two glasses. Meanwhile* CARMENCITA *has gone up to* CARDURA, *put down her tray, and poured him a glass of wine.*

CARMENCITA (*offering it timidly*). Señor——

CARDURA (*half-humorously*). This is looting——

CARMENCITA. Señor Castro owes you more than a glass of wine.

CARDURA (*taking it*). Well, the day is hot enough.

[LEÓN *has taken up a glass and helped herself. She and* CARDURA *drink.*

RODRIGUEZ (*to* CONSUELO). I'm not used to being refused by women.

CONSUELO (*calmly*). Are you not?
[*She moves deliberately to him. He hands her a glass.*

RODRIGUEZ (*pleased with himself*). I thought you would. Good girl! We'll drink to your beauty—— (CONSUELO *throws the contents of her glass into his face. He starts back, then darts at her, gripping her wrists.*) Ah, vixen—would you——

59

TERESA (*meanwhile, alarmed and scandalized*). Señorita !

[RODRIGUEZ *gets an arm about* CONSUELO *and forces her to drink a little of his wine. She wrenches herself away from him, panting, and smacks his face. He laughs, roused now and, fascinated by her, catches her in his arms and kisses her passionately, forcing her response.* TERESA *meanwhile continues in great agitation :*

Oh ! We should not have come ! I said we should not ! They'll shoot us and worse—and then what will your aunt say ?

CARDURA (*meanwhile*). Rodriguez ! What the hell are you playing at ?

RODRIGUEZ (*panting*). Hell—yes—with a pretty little she-devil—— (*This is where he kisses* CONSUELO.)

TERESA. Holy Mother, preserve us ! And she who has been kissed by a duke——

[CONSUELO *has liked the kiss and is now definitely attracted to* RODRIGUEZ. *She has recovered her poise, and looks into* RODRIGUEZ' *eyes provocatively. He is the more overcome.*

CONSUELO (*mischievously*). And whose will is the stronger now ? You may lead bulls, but who leads matadors ?

RODRIGUEZ (*thickly*). Ah ! Beautiful——

TERESA (*with a fluttering attempt to assert herself*). Señorita ! Remember that I am here——

CONSUELO (*laughing*). But he doesn't want to kiss you.

TERESA. And it's daylight and a public place—and a lady remembers her behaviour—even if there is a war on——

[*The* 1ST REPUBLICAN SOLDIER *runs on* R. *All turn to him.*

CARDURA. What is it ?

1ST REPUBLICAN SOLDIER. The prisoner—that Castro ! He has escaped——

RODRIGUEZ (*furiously*). Escaped ? Imbecile !——

1st Republican Soldier (*to* Cardura). It was your fault, señor. You said there was to be no accident to him——

Cardura. I didn't tell you to let him go. And one so fat——

1st Republican Soldier (*very quickly*). But what would you? He broke away, slippery as an eel. We dared not shoot, because of what you said. The devil lent wings to his feet, and he ran like a wild beast of Portugal into a side street, a warren of houses. Pedro is still looking for him. Oh, I assure you, señor comrade, that it was your unfortunate and certainly hell-inspired order——

Cardura (*cutting him short*). Silence!

[Rodriguez, *flushed by success in love, works himself into a fine rage to show off further to* Consuelo. *He moves away from her, advancing slowly on the* Soldier.

Rodriguez (*to* Cardura). It is as I said, Cardura. (*To the* Soldier.) And you, offal, dare to come back here with such a tale? Are you a soldier of the Republic?

1st Republican Soldier (*losing his impudence*). But, señor——

Rodriguez (*interrupting*). Pah! I know you! To-morrow—everything can be done to-morrow, nothing finished to-day. If nature hadn't been stronger than your trollop of a mother, she'd have left off bearing you until to-morrow——

1st Republican Soldier (*turning nasty*). Señor, I am a good son of the Republic, in which one man is the equal of another. I do not submit to insults——

Rodriguez. You will submit to what I choose. One man the equal of another, is he? You are the equal of no more than the ditch-got spawn of a Gypsy——

1st Republican Soldier. And am I to bear such things? You insult my mother and offend my pride. (*To* Cardura.) You heard him, señor——

Cardura (*curtly*). Enough of this! Get back to your fellow, and find the man.

1ST REPUBLICAN SOLDIER. But it is a maze—a rabbit-warren. It would need a company——

CARDURA. Find him. I've no more men to spare.

1ST REPUBLICAN SOLDIER. He has insulted me. I wish to make proper complaint of it. Who is he to confuse my mother with his own?

RODRIGUEZ (*starting*). Ah, you insolent rat—— (*He draws his pistol.*)

CARDURA. Rodriguez!

LEÓN (*amused, encouraging*). Aha!

TERESA
CARMENCITA } (*Scream.*)

CONSUELO. (*Laughs softly.*)

1ST REPUBLICAN SOLDIER (*losing his dignity, frightened*). I go, señor—I go!

[*He runs off* R. RODRIGUEZ *turns back to* CONSUELO, *pleased with himself.* CARDURA *shrugs wearily and, unslinging his field-glasses, turns upstage and surveys the country.*

RODRIGUEZ (*to* CONSUELO). I am not to be trifled with.

CONSUELO (*provocatively*). I always trifle with men like you. (*Turning away from him.*) You will send me a jar of fresh oil. I shall expect it. Come, Teresa.

TERESA. This is a business to be mixed up in! There's no respectability in war, nowadays.

RODRIGUEZ (*to* CONSUELO). I shall come with you to your house. There are soldiers about.

CONSUELO (*her voice cool, but her eyes provocative*). Oh! Do you call them *soldiers*?

RODRIGUEZ (*between anger and admiration*). Only a bullet would stop your tongue—(*admiration winning*)—or another kiss.

CONSUELO (*laughing*). You'd best economize with your—bullets.

TERESA. Oh!

[RODRIGUEZ *suddenly and possessively puts his arm about* CONSUELO *and leads her off* L. TERESA *gasps in futile indignation.*

LEÓN (*sardonically*). And that's all the difference between a lady and a woman.

[LEÓN *takes the bottle and her glass down to one of the tables and sits, drinking.* TERESA *goes quickly to* CARDURA.

TERESA. Señor officer——

[CARDURA *takes no notice.* TERESA *taps him on the shoulder. He swings round.*

CARDURA. What is it now? I tell you there is no olive oil——

TERESA (*plaintively*). But I don't want olive oil——

LEÓN (*laughing*). She wants you to go home with her, señor. (TERESA *starts.*) But you can find a younger one——

TERESA. How dare you, woman! (*To* CARDURA.) He —that man—has gone off with the señorita——

CARDURA (*shortly*). Then you'd better go after them, to see they don't get into mischief. (LEÓN *laughs.*) It takes two to make that sort of love.

[*He turns away from her.* TERESA *stands for a moment, beyond words, then turns and stalks off* L.

TERESA (*as she goes*). In the old days, we knew what was right and what was wrong. But we had the King then——

LA BORRACHERA (*entering* L., *meeting* TERESA). And of a certainty he showed you what was *wrong*——

[*She makes a face at* TERESA, *who hurries off* L. *Then she goes down to* LEÓN's *table and sits, continuing :*

Right—wrong—oh, the war! One minute we shoot, the next we kiss. One day we salute with the raised hand—(*she does so*)—live, Franco! The next we salute with the clenched fist—(*she does so*)—up with communism!

63

LEÓN. Spain wants neither. I am a good anarchist. I believe in life without law. (*Noticing that* LA BORRACHERA *has stolen her bottle, quickly changing her tone.*) Here, you old thief!

[LA BORRACHERA *has a good drink before surrendering the bottle. The* PADRE *has re-entered R. and has heard the last lines. He moves over to them, sad and stern.*

LA BORRACHERA (*half-drunk, laughing*). For me, I've always had one worthy ambition—to get drunk on good wine.

LEÓN. You're near it.

LA BORRACHERA. Not I—I'm still merry. I've a notable head, I tell you. When you hear me begin to sing psalms—— (*She sees the* PADRE *and breaks off nervously.*)

PADRE. Anarchy—drunkenness—bawdry. Don't you think you should be ashamed of yourselves?

LEÓN. Ashamed? What have I to be ashamed of? They ruined my man's vineyard and they murdered him. All my life I was a good daughter of the Church —(*bitterly*) for that, only for that.

PADRE. My daughter, the Church has her own sorrows —as her Master had.

LEÓN (*half-awed by inbred respect, but trying to assert herself*). You're lucky that he (*indicating* CARDURA'S *back*) took this place. There are many nowadays who do not like priests.

LA BORRACHERA (*also awed*). Be quiet, gossip! He may still have power. (*In drunken confidence.*) Best be on both sides, then you're safe. (*Louder.*) And who doubts that the Church had uses. For three years the sisters of the Sacred Heart looked to my bad leg. Now it must tend itself.

PADRE (*humorously, matter-of-fact like a family doctor*). What your leg needs is fresh water, clean bandages, no more wine—and a good deal more prayer. Go home and see to it—and set a better example to others.

LA BORRACHERA (*amused*). I? Example? And should I set myself up, at my age, to be an example? (*She laughs, then breaks off, superstitious fear uppermost, rising nervously.*) Don't look at me like that, Father! I'm only a poor old woman who does no harm—you like your little joke, too——

PADRE (*dryly*). You're a poor old woman who does a great deal of harm—mainly to herself. Now be off with you, both of you, and let's have no more of this wild talk. (*To* LEÓN.) Anarchy, indeed! You're safer off the streets to-day. And don't forget it's a long time since I heard your confession.

LEÓN (*truculently*). I get along well enough without it.

PADRE (*challengingly*). Are you certain of that?

[*He looks steadily at her. She drops her eyes and turns away, subdued.* LA BORRACHERA, *thoroughly uneasy, grips her arm and they go off L. The* PADRE *looks sadly after them.*

They'll be as bad again to-morrow. Like ignorant children—wandering in the darkness of war.

[CARMENCITA, *who has been listening to the* PADRE, *crosses to downstage L. and slips off, curtsying to the* PADRE *as she goes.*

CARDURA (*who has turned*). Your people made that darkness.

PADRE. All people are my people. The Church is outside party politics. But the Republic has done great harm to the Church.

CARDURA. The Republic saw that the Church was used by the rich to exploit the poor. Can you wonder that the poor now attack you?

PADRE. I do not wonder at anything the poor do. I've lived a long life with them and I know them. They have no thought but for the moment—the moment of kneeling before God—(*sadly*)—or the moment of burning a church.

CARDURA. Can you deny that they've been oppressed?

PADRE. My son, I am here to preach the gospel of God. I am here to help where I can. Not only the poor cry out for help. Poverty is not the only burden. And God's own Son was oppressed. Do you suppose God intended that life should be easy for anyone?

CARDURA. I don't suppose anything about God. And you are on the side of the rich.

PADRE (*hurt, but not offended*). Rich? I don't think that you, a poet, regard riches—material things—as of the greatest importance.

CARDURA. I've given up poetry for what I believe— (*with a sudden sincerity, under the* PADRE's *quiet gaze*)—or as near as I can get to it.

PADRE. Politics—revolutions—I've not time to mix in them, even if I understood them, which I do not. My sphere of action is limited—(*chuckling*)—but there's unlimited work in it.

CARDURA. You read Mass to Franco's men before we drove them out.

PADRE. I'd do the same for yours, if they asked me. I wish they would.

CARDURA. You'd do more good by telling me the number of the enemy, and what you know of their plans.

PADRE. I shall not do that.

CARDURA. But you'd tell them of ours.

PADRE. No.

[*Pause.* CARDURA *stares at the* PADRE.

CARDURA. I believe you. I beg your pardon, Father. You earn respect, however old-fashioned your ideas.

PADRE. God Himself, perhaps, is a little old-fashioned in His ideas. (*He has moved up to near* CARDURA, *and now indicates the view off backstage.*) There's nothing very modern about all this—thanks to Him.

CARDURA. Except the enemy artillery hidden over there (*points off to R. backstage*) and the German bombers that will be over presently.

PADRE (*wearily*). Ah—machines of war ! (*Wistfully.*)
But, just for the moment, here in this place they are
silent. For the moment we may breathe and refresh
ourselves. You are still a poet, and you have written
of this beauty—of Castile.

CARDURA. I am a Castilian of Aranjuez. Castile is the
heart of Spain. (*Fiercely.*) Your rebels may have taken
Estremadura and most of Andalusia. They may have
spread themselves in the North. But they have con-
quered neither the land nor the spirit of Castile. We
bar the road towards Toledo, and Toledo guards
Madrid. They shall not pass to Madrid.

PADRE (*gently*). I spoke of other things. Are you so little
of a poet now ? The beauty of this upland country has
an austerity more pleasing than the fatness of valleys.
Don't you think so ?

CARDURA (*in a gentler tone*). Yes. I once wrote this—or
another man in my skin wrote it :

[*He turns downstage to face the* PADRE, *who is standing a
little behind him. For a moment the poet in him drives out
everything else as he recites :*

" I have seen the reflections of clouds along the table-
lands
In the impact of June sun, turning the wheat
To a viridian and strange sea, reaching
League on league toward horizons hard and high
And definite as death. Upon that sea
The burnt-brick shapes of churches ride like ships,
The tongues of their bells in the heavy bell-towers
rolling,
Tolling along the spaces, calling the traveller
From point to point of his purpose, under the wide
sky.
And I have seen Castile in another colour
When the green has gone with the harvest, and
lean peasants,
Their sickles laid aside at threshing-time,
With girls and women, burnt as antique figures
On some Greek vase, move on the beaten floors,

Tossing a haze of glittering chaff that smokes
Above the stark blond fields and leaves the grain
In metalled heaps——"

[*He breaks off suddenly at the crack of a rifle-shot off to
R. backstage. Instantly alert, he swings round, gripping his
field-glasses.*

That was from the valley——

PADRE (*following his gaze*). As though someone fired at
this cliff——

CARDURA. But—— (*Looking over the precipice, pointing.*)
Yes! Look! Someone's climbing up——

PADRE. Up this precipice! Madness! Two hundred
feet and almost sheer——

CARDURA. He's nearly up it, though. There's a sort of
chimney. I say—it's a girl! She'll never make the
last bit.

[CARDURA *runs off downstage L. into the inn, to return
in a moment with a length of rope. He rapidly tests one of the
posts of the railing and makes the rope fast, then ties a bowline
about himself and slips over the edge. A few more shots, of
which no one takes any notice, and scrambling sounds off.*

PADRE. Be careful—— (*He stands, tense, looking over,
then:*) There's a rock a little to the left of your left
foot—that's it. (*Pause.*) Now wait on that ledge for
her. She's just—— (*In surprise.*) Why—it's little Soledad!——

CARDURA (*off*). Right! I've got you. Get hold of this
rope. Now stay here, and I'll pull you up——

SOLEDAD (*off, breathless but definite*). I can—manage——

CARDURA (*off*). Up with you, then.

[*More scrambling, off. A moment later* SOLEDAD VALLINA
pulls herself over the edge. The PADRE *assists her. She lies
on the ground, panting. She is a young girl, dressed in dirty
overalls or shirt and slacks, torn and dishevelled. In spite of
her appearance, character and intelligence are evident in her.*
CARDURA *follows her after a moment.*

PADRE. Soledad! You——

SOLEDAD (*sitting up, speaking with difficulty*). A minute—my stomach's turning over and over and—the world's swinging round and round——

CARDURA (*gently, appreciating her courage*). I should think so. Only a fool or a mountaineer would attempt a climb like that.

SOLEDAD. It isn't so bad as it looks——

CARDURA. Come farther away from the edge.

[*He lifts her in his arms and helps her downstage L. to a chair at one of the tables. The* PADRE *finds one of the bottles of wine and a glass.* SOLEDAD, *recovering her breath, drinks from the bottle with appreciation.*

SOLEDAD. Ah ! That's good——

CARDURA. Who are you ? Why did you do a damn-fool thing like that ?

SOLEDAD. It was the only way in. I couldn't get across the bridge—and it's urgent. You are the commandante ?

CARDURA. Yes. Miguel Cardura.

SOLEDAD. That's right. That's what they told me. Look. (*She takes a small badge from a pocket and shows him, concealing it in her hand so that the* PADRE *does not see it. He nods. She indicates the* PADRE.) Send him away. He's an enemy.

PADRE (*hurt*). I am not your enemy, my child. (*To* CARDURA.) She is of this village. She was one of my most regular communicants before she went to Madrid.

SOLEDAD (*curtly*). Please ! This is war—and *we* didn't make it.

CARDURA (*almost apologetically*). Perhaps, if you wouldn't mind, Father——

PADRE. Very well, my son. (*With a sad smile, shaking his head.*) There is more than death in this business of war. (*Pulling himself together.*) I'll go and look in at my hospital. It's about time I did.

[*He goes off L.*

SOLEDAD. You let him go where he likes?

CARDURA. Of course. You ought to know he's a good old man.

SOLEDAD (*appraising him*). Can you find time for softness?

CARDURA (*curtly*). No. Only for common sense. He's as good as a doctor.

SOLEDAD (*momentarily thoughtful*). I used to love him, but —(*harshly*)—the Church means Franco now, and who can think of God and Franco together. So one hates, now.

CARDURA. You're very young.

SOLEDAD (*flashing at him*). Don't be a fool! No one is young in these days. The very babies are old in knowledge of death. (*For a moment her eyes fill with pain, then she shrugs.*) But individuals don't matter. Most of us will be dead soon, anyway. Only Spain matters—the Republic. (*She jumps to her feet, urgent again.*) Listen —I've been down in the valley, among their soldiers——

CARDURA. What?

SOLEDAD. They're determined to get this place back. They've brought up a fresh regiment of infantry and two more batteries, as well as engineers—(*she runs backstage, pointing off R.*)—into the woods down there. (CARDURA *moves up to her, looking through his field-glasses in the direction she indicates.*) I've been watching them come up.

CARDURA. They're well hidden.

SOLEDAD. They came up at dawn, through the woods— over that ridge, mainly. I knew you couldn't see them, so——

CARDURA. So you risked your life. Thank you.

SOLEDAD. You'll thank me by keeping those swine out of here.

[CARDURA *has taken a pad and pencil from his pocket and is scribbling a note.*

CARDURA (*as he writes*). We'll keep 'em out. We're dangerously thin along this side, but the bridge is mined ready for blowing and it's the only way across that ravine.

SOLEDAD. Then why haven't you blown it?

CARDURA. Because I've had hopes of another advance, but no means of building another bridge.

SOLEDAD. They left it for the same reason, I suppose. But they could build another.

CARDURA. They'd find it expensive to try. We've got to hold this place. (*With more passion.*) It's a question of time—time—time! We're a comparative rabble fighting a trained army. We've got to have time to pull ourselves together. And this ridge, strongly held (*gestures R. and L.*) will give us a little of it. Wait a moment. I must send this message. (*He goes off quickly L., calling as he goes:*) Here, Juan—Juan——

[SOLEDAD *remains thoughtfully looking off. In a moment* CARDURA *returns.*

SOLEDAD. Are things going so badly?

CARDURA (*looking straight at her*). You're a brave girl.

SOLEDAD (*impatiently*). Oh, hell! I asked you a question. If I'd no right, tell me off. I don't want compliments —or evasions.

CARDURA (*coldly*). I was about to pay you the compliment of saying that you'd earned the right to be told the truth. (*Pause, then:*) This is between us two. Things in general are going so badly that we've just got to ignore how badly they're going.

SOLEDAD (*quietly, looking steadily at him*). I see. Thank you. (*Pause.*) That was a strange phrase for a soldier.

CARDURA. I'm not a soldier. I'm a poet.

SOLEDAD. A poet! Of course! I wondered why I knew your name. Miguel Cardura. I was doing modern Spanish poets in my arts degree work at the University of Madrid. (*Bitterly.*) Just think of that—six months ago. (*She laughs and shrugs.*) Have you time to give me a cigarette?

CARDURA. Of course. (*He fumbles for cigarettes, not taking his eyes off her.*) I'd like to do more than that, señorita. I'd like to say that I admire your devotion—(*as she makes another impatient gesture*)—no, listen to me! There's no time for easy approaches, nowadays—not much grace in anything—but I want you to know that I've never met anyone I wanted so much to meet a second time. There's something in you——

SOLEDAD (*staring at him in wonder*). But I—I'm filthy and all torn to bits and—— (*She breaks off, gulps, and continues angrily :*) Do you want to make me cry?

CARDURA (*putting his hands on her arms in a friendly gesture*). I want you to promise that, if we both get out of this mess, you'll meet me again.

SOLEDAD (*responding, smiling, but nervous and uncertain*). I liked your poetry a lot.

CARDURA. I'd rather you liked me.

SOLEDAD. I—think I might. (*He kisses her lightly, then releases her. She continues gravely :*) But I don't think there'll be much afterwards for us.

[*For a moment they look steadily at each other, then he smiles.*

CARDURA. Well, we've met, anyway, and that's a beginning. Here's your cigarette.

SOLEDAD. Thank you.

[*He lights her cigarette and one for himself.*

CARDURA. Eaten anything lately?

SOLEDAD. No.

CARDURA (*going downstage L., calling*). Carmencita!

SOLEDAD. It doesn't matter. You've other things to think of.

CARDURA. I've advised headquarters. I can do no more until the fun begins.

[CARMENCITA *enters downstage L.*

CARMENCITA. You called, señor?

CARDURA. Can you find this young lady some food?

CARMENCITA. Why, Soledad! Yes, of course—what there is.

[CARMENCITA *goes off downstage L. The drone of an aeroplane is heard.* CARDURA *and* SOLEDAD *look up.*

CARDURA. Ah! One of theirs. I'll have to go. You get some food, and keep out of the way of things.

SOLEDAD (*mutinously*). Like hell I will——

CARDURA (*urgently*). I mean that. I don't want you hurt. See you later!

[*He pats her shoulder and runs off R. The noise of the aeroplane grows louder. One or two small bombs are heard at a little distance.* SOLEDAD, *staring after* CARDURA, *takes no notice of them. She suddenly begins to cry, putting her hands to her face.* CARMENCITA *runs on downstage L.*

CARMENCITA. Soledad—wouldn't you like to come inside and eat? It's safer. They're bombing us again. (*Surprised.*) Why—you're crying!

SOLEDAD (*dashing away her tears, sniffing, indignantly*). I am not crying. I—it's the dust from the cliff——

[LA BORRACHERA *hurries on L.*

LA BORRACHERA. They're at it again! What'll become of us all?

CARMENCITA. Come inside with me.

LA BORRACHERA. Not I. If the sky's going to come down on me, it must. I'll not have stones as well. Besides, an old woman has her curiosity.

[*The whine and explosion of shells begins off R. and increases during the following scene.*

SOLEDAD. They've started. Never mind the food. Come and help.

[SOLEDAD *runs off R.*

LA BORRACHERA. Help? What's she going to do—fire a gun? I wouldn't know how—but I know one thing—— (*She lifts her skirt and takes a wicked-looking knife from her garter.*) I can slit a throat or two.

[LEÓN *runs on L., with other* VILLAGERS *if desired. They group to R., looking off.* RODRIGUEZ *runs on L. and off R.* Why don't they blow the bridge?

LEÓN. All in good time—when some of the swine have ventured on it.

[*Machine-gun fire now mingles with the sound of the artillery at a little distance off R.* CONSUELO *runs on L., excited.* TERESA, *frightened, follows her.*

TERESA (*panting*). Señorita—have you no sense of decorum?

[*They join the others. The sounds of war are now louder. The aeroplane returns, zooming nearer, dropping one or two more bombs. Those on stage duck as the bombs fall.*

LA BORRACHERA (*looking up*). That's German. A nice thing, to drop such nastiness on respectable civilians! (*Waving her knife at the sky.*) You come down here, young man. I'll show you!

TERESA (*pulling* CONSUELO'S *sleeve*). Señorita! For the love of God, let us join your aunt in the cellar.

CONSUELO (*excited*). Join her if you wish. I'm staying here. This is better than a bull-fight.

LA BORRACHERA (*cackling, digging her in the ribs*). Better than any bull-fight that fancy young man of yours ever made. Is he coming back to you when it's dark and your aunt's in bed?

[CONSUELO *draws herself haughtily away.*

LEÓN (*harshly*). Quiet! (*Anxiously.*) Why hasn't that bridge been blown?

[CASTRO, *terrified, panting, runs on R., scattering the women. He is dashing off L. when* LA BORRACHERA *grabs him.* RODRIGUEZ *runs on R. with his pistol in his hand, in an almost hysterical state of excitement.*

LA BORRACHERA. Not so fast——

LEÓN. Why isn't the bridge blown?

RODRIGUEZ (*shouting*). Why isn't the bridge blown—ha?

I'll tell you that. (*He fires at* CASTRO's *feet, making him squeal and jump into the air.*) You see him—the traitor——

[*He snatches the knife from* LA BORRACHERA *and begins to edge towards the terrified* CASTRO, *driving him step by step upstage towards the edge of the cliff, jabbing him with the knife, drawing little squeals of terror from him, dancing on his toes from side to side. All watch them, fascinated, except* CARMENCITA, *who has covered her face with her hands.*

RODRIGUEZ *talks meanwhile.*

I knew—I, Alvaro Rodriguez. But we've a fool in command. I saw this Castro, skulking up the ravine. They pull the switch—there is no explosion. And why? (*Pointing at* CASTRO.) He has killed the sentry and cut the wires.

LA BORRACHERA. Mother of God!

LEÓN. The traitor!

CARMENCITA. Then—we are lost——

[CASTRO *has now been driven to near the edge where the rail is broken. The guns have stopped, but machine-gun fire is nearer.*

RODRIGUEZ (*savagely*). This is no bull to play, friends. He will not charge at all.

CASTRO. Jesu! Have pity!

[*He is on the edge before he realizes it, topples, tries to recover his balance, leaning back with his arms flailing.* RODRIGUEZ *laughs, lunges forward, and pushes him over. He screams and falls, his scream long-drawn, dying away.* RODRIGUEZ *looks over for a moment, with* LA BORRACHERA, *who has run upstage.* RODRIGUEZ *laughs again.* LA BORRACHERA *turns away with a shudder.* RODRIGUEZ *runs off R. Almost immediately, however, he backs on again, firing his pistol repeatedly off R. Rifle-shots reply, and machine-gun fire is intensified. The others scatter to cover on either side of the R. entrance.* RODRIGUEZ, *having fired his last shot, savagely throws his pistol off R. and turns to run. He is shot in the back and spins round, falling dead towards downstage L. If desired, a few* REPUBLICAN SOLDIERS *can run on R. and off L., in flight.* CONSUELO *screams at* RODRIGUEZ' *fall and hurries to him. The* PADRE *hurries on L., anxiously.*

PADRE. Have they——

[*He is interrupted by the entrance of* TWO REBEL SOLDIERS *to R. They are in uniform and carry rifles at the ready. They enter quickly, but with caution, alert for traps.*

1ST REBEL SOLDIER. Back—all of you. Over there.

[*The* SOLDIERS *sweep the others to downstage L. in a huddled group, except the* PADRE, *who is now upstage L.*

Keep quite still or you'll be shot.

CARMENCITA (*gasping with fear*). Aaah !

2ND REBEL SOLDIER (*leering at her*). Don't you worry, my pretty. (*Significantly.*) We'll find a use for you.

[*The battle noises off R. have died down, and now cease. Bring up the sound of marching feet, off R.*

VOICE OF N.C.O. (*off*). Halt ! Right turn !

[*The marching stops.*

LA BORRACHERA (*looking off to R.*). They're here—already——

[*The* SOLDIERS *spring to attention.* COLONEL PHILIP ADAJA *enters R. He is very smart and quite cool and unemotional. If desired he may be accompanied by other* OFFICERS *and* SOLDIERS *of the rebel army, in uniform. He glances about him, then salutes the* PADRE.

ADAJA. Back again, Father. (*As the* PADRE *takes no notice.*) You're glad to see me, I suppose ?

PADRE. I'd rather see an end to this war.

ADAJA. We'll arrange that as soon as possible. You'll be pleased to hear we've got the leader of this little lot.

PADRE (*starting*). The leader ?

ADAJA (*to the* SOLDIERS). Bring Cardura here.

[*The* SOLDIERS *go off R. and return in a moment with* CARDURA *between them. He is dishevelled and his right arm hangs useless, the hand covered with blood.* ADAJA *sits*

76

on the box, as CARDURA *did at the beginning of the play.
The others watch tensely.*

CARMENCITA. Your hand! Oh, look at your hand!
(*She stops, frightened.*)

ADAJA (*to* CARDURA). You were in command of the
rebels here.

CARDURA. I was in command here. The rebels are all
on your side.

ADAJA. We won't argue about that. I can't congratu-
late you on your defence of this place.

CARDURA (*quietly*). Your own, yesterday, wasn't so good.
But you managed to get away with a whole skin.

ADAJA. Are you being insolent?

CARDURA (*coolly*). Not at all. I was merely referring to
your superior organization.

[SOLEDAD *runs on R., stopping with a gasp as she sees*
CARDURA.

ADAJA. To do you justice, you'd poor material and too
little of it. Otherwise you'd obviously have had a
second line of defence. But enough of that. You are
not a soldier. Your men are not soldiers. Therefore
you will not be treated as prisoners of war. (*Pause.*
CARDURA *looks straight at him.*) You expected this?

CARDURA. From butchers, one expects butchery.

ADAJA. I am not a butcher.

CARDURA. No—just a butcher's assistant.

PADRE (*alarmed*). My son—be careful——

CARDURA. That wouldn't make any difference, Father.

ADAJA. You're right. We'll not waste any more time.
(*To the* SOLDIERS.) Take him away.

SOLEDAD (*crying out*). No, no!

[*She takes a few quick steps towards* CARDURA. ADAJA
looks at her with sudden interest.

ADAJA. Aha! So you've turned up again? The little
spy.

SPANISH RHAPSODY

CARDURA. She is not a spy.

ADAJA. Oh, yes, she is. I know her quite well. She should have been caught this morning.

CARDURA. No! She's only a village girl here. (*To the* PADRE.) Tell them——

PADRE. That is true. I can vouch for her.

ADAJA (*cynically*). Why, Father—do you want to destroy my faith in the honesty of the Church?

PADRE. My son——

ADAJA (*interrupting*). Don't lie to me. (*To the* SOLDIERS.) Take her along with him and the rest.

CARMENCITA. (*Screams.*)

PADRE. What are you going to do?

ADAJA. Shoot them, of course.

PADRE. But that would be murder! (*Desperately.*) You are a Christian——

ADAJA. Naturally. What's that to do with it?

PADRE. You need to ask, with hatred breaking all bounds?

ADAJA (*still quite cool*). I'm not satisfying any hatred. I'm doing my duty. This rabble against us must be exterminated, for the sake of Spain.

CARDURA. Thanks, Father. Don't waste any more breath on my account. (*To* ADAJA.) But you must take my word that this girl has nothing to do with us. She is not a spy.

ADAJA. Silence!

PADRE (*appealing to* ADAJA). Is it to be said that he (*indicating* CARDURA) is more merciful than you? He spared a man's life this morning, at my request. And *he* professes no religion.

ADAJA (*sternly*). Father Diez—do you want me to report you for suspected bolshevik sympathies?

PADRE (*sternly*). You may report me for what you will. (*With authority.*) In the name of Christ and His Church, I command you to show mercy to these prisoners.

ADAJA (*coolly*). One more word from you, and I'll shoot you along with them.

[SOLEDAD *goes quietly to* CARDURA, *standing by him.*

SOLEDAD. There is no mercy in brutes who tear their own country apart for the satisfaction of their greed. You fight to restore riches to the rich ; to tread the poor into greater poverty. But we fight for better things than that. We've right on our side, and humanity, and love of liberty. You may spread your fascism over Spain—over the world—but you won't be allowed for long to halt the wheels of progress. Live, freedom !

[ADAJA *takes no notice. He is taking out papers from his pocket. Without looking up, he gestures to the* SOLDIERS.

ADAJA. Off with them.

[CARDURA *smiles at* SOLEDAD, *who smiles back at him and reaches out her hand to his left hand. The* SOLDIERS *close in on them and they go off quietly* R. CARMENCITA *is crying. The others watch in silent and fearful fascination.*

PADRE. Then I will go, to be with them.

ADAJA (*reading papers*). Stay where you are.

PADRE. She was a communicant. If she desires—if they desire—my ministrations——

[*He begins to move* R. ADAJA *jumps up.*

ADAJA (*coldly*). If you take another step I'll shoot twenty more of your villagers. These bolshevik animals need no sacrament.

[*The* PADRE *stops. For a moment he stands in silence.* ADAJA *sits again and returns to his papers. The* PADRE, *realizing that he can do nothing more, clasps his hands and begins to pray.*

PADRE. Misereatur vestri omnipotens Deus, et dimissis peccatis vestris, perducat vos ad vitam aeternam.

[*As he begins to pray, the women on stage one by one drop to their knees. First* CARMENCITA, *who is sobbing quietly, then* CONSUELO *and* TERESA *with any* SUPERS, *then* LA

BORRACHERA, *last of all* LEÓN. *The* PADRE *goes on, calmly :*

Indulgentiam, absolutionem,——

[*A shattering volley of rifle fire from off R. The* PADRE *continues, still calm :*

et remissionem peccatorum nostrorum, tribuat nobis omnipotens et misericors Dominus.

[*Slow curtain during the last line, so that while the* PADRE *is still speaking,*

THE CURTAIN FALLS

T. B. MORRIS

If Imagination Amend Them

A Play in One Act

LONDON
FREDERICK MULLER LTD.
29 Great James Street, W.C.1

FIRST PUBLISHED BY FREDERICK MULLER, LTD.
IN 1948
PRINTED IN GREAT BRITAIN BY WYMAN & SONS LTD.
LONDON, READING AND FAKENHAM

" The best in this kind are but shadows ; and the worst are no worse, if imagination amend them."

A Midsummer Night's Dream.

If Imagination Amend Them was first presented by the
Harrodian Club (London) at the Welwyn Drama Festival
on 25th May, 1937, with the following cast :

Inspiration	..	..	..	PEGGY CHASE
The Writer	..	..	..	RICHARD SHARPE
Thalia ..	..	..	..	DORIS HOMEWOOD
Erato ..	..	..	..	GWEN GREY
Euterpe ..	..	..	..	NORAH O'DELL
Calliope ..	..	..	..	EILEEN MILTON
Melpomene	..	..	..	MARJORIE HODSON
The Girl ..	..	..	..	RITA HALL
The Tormentor	..	..	..	NOEL MOSS
The Hero	..	..	..	MAURICE QUICK
The Heroine	..	..	..	CONNIE FRASER
The Villain	..	..	..	JOHN HARDIMAN
Frustration	..	..	..	ALEXANDER HAZELL
Necessity ..	..	..	..	ROBERT LAURENCE
Propaganda	..	..	..	BRENDON ARTHUR
Sentimentality	..	..	..	EDITH HENDRA

The play produced by
WILLIAM CLEMENTS and JOHN YOUNG

THE CHARACTERS

INSPIRATION.
THE WRITER.
THALIA, *the Comic Muse.*
ERATO, *the Muse of Love and Mimicry.*
EUTERPE, *the Lyric Muse.*
CALLIOPE, *the Epic Muse.*
MELPOMENE, *the Tragic Muse.*
THE GIRL.
THE TORMENTOR.
THE HERO.
THE HEROINE.
THE VILLAIN.
FRUSTRATION.
NECESSITY.
PROPAGANDA.
SENTIMENTALITY.

THE SCENE

A writer's room. The action takes place largely in the mind of the writer.

SETTING AND PRODUCTION NOTES

THE following notes upon the setting and dressing of this comedy are merely suggestions. It may be left to the Producer's imagination and affords the widest possible scope, as it may be produced either simply or with fantastic elaboration.

Some of the players may wear masks, or be made up to resemble masks, or neither, as desired. A background of suitably varied music, especially for the MUSES, the three sketches, and the final scene, is strongly recommended. Variation of the general lighting, to accord with the different moods of the play, will also add considerably to its effect. For the most part the action should be fast, " large ", and exaggerated. Exceptions, such as the more serious lines of the MUSES, the final scene, etc., will be easily apparent.

A curtain set should be used. Backstage C. is a gigantic, possibly eccentric, question-mark, of cardboard painted in a striking pattern of bright colours and fixed to the curtains. It reaches as high as the vision of the audience permits. To one side of it is fixed a tragic mask, to the other side a comic mask, also done in large, bold, eccentric style.

From C.R. to backstage R. there are steps leading to a rostrum on which is a throne-like seat. Backstage, towards L., is a chest, containing the properties described later, and with a mirror somewhere handy to help the players to prepare for the brief sketches. The chest might also be painted in colours, and be labelled PROPS in large, eccentric letters. Downstage L. is a desk, with a reading-lamp and the usual writing materials, including a pile of blank paper. Above the desk is a screen, which rather suggests the isolation of this corner of the stage, but must not interfere with movements to and from the desk. A chair faces the desk, so that anyone using it has his right profile to the audience and his back to most of the stage. A wastepaper basket is downstage of the desk.

Entrances are downstage R. and upstage L. But it may be arranged that the figures of the fantasy enter at various points, between the curtains.

The light from the reading lamp should be of different quality from that of the rest of the stage. The desk and its immediate surroundings are reality, the remainder exists only in the WRITER's imagination ; first in his subconscious, then in his conscious mind.

IF IMAGINATION AMEND THEM

As the Curtain rises INSPIRATION *is sitting on the throne. She is a young and beautiful girl. She will have nothing to say, but her beauty and grace are essential. Her dress might be ivory in colour, of a heavy material that closely moulds her limbs, and she might have a striking head-dress, perhaps of a dull gold colour. This head-dress might include a mask, but if so it should be a very beautiful one. Until towards the end of the play, however, she is entirely covered, head-dress and all, by a veil of some filmy material, and sits rigidly in a statuesque pose.*

The WRITER, *an intense-looking young man in dark clothes is sitting at the desk, staring at the blank paper before him, playing with his pen (which is a quill), ruffling his hair, and so on. He does not look towards* INSPIRATION, *because she is inside his mind.*

THALIA, ERATO, EUTERPE, CALLIOPE *and* MELPOMENE *enter R., quietly. They are women as nearly as possible of the same size. All their movements are graceful, like a slow dance. Their manner varies from* THALIA'S *comedy to* MELPOMENE'S *tragedy ; their voices and colouring could also be varied, from a soprano and blonde* THALIA *to a contralto and brunette* MELPOMENE. *They might wear Grecian dresses and wigs, with facial make-up to resemble masks. The colour of their dresses could be uniform, or could be in a range of dull matt shades such as gold, rose, blue, purple and black. Or a monochrome range from light to dark would be effective. They*

89

*move on and stand R. in an oblique line up and down stage,
looking towards the* WRITER, *who of course takes no notice
of them, and speaking together.*

MUSES. Five of us here you have called—five of the Nine.
  Deep from your soul you have called ; in your mind
    we are here ;
  Daughters of Jupiter, daughters of Mnemosyne. . . .
  Far have we journeyed from god-haunted peaks of
    Parnassus ;
  We, the companions of gods, to give aid to your
    questing. . . .

  [*With a change of rhythm.*

  Lovely and remote is Inspiration,
  Demanding all, and giving all again
  Through the twin ecstasies of Joy and Pain.

  [*Continuing separately, each as she speaks holding out her
  arms towards the* WRITER'S *back.*

MELPOMENE. I am Melpomene. I bring to birth
  High tragedy——

CALLIOPE. The record of great deeds
  Do I, Calliope, in epics urge——

EUTERPE. I am Euterpe. Mine a gentler prompting
  Towards a more limpid verse and lyrical——

ERATO. Erato is my name, and what are these (*indicating
    the others*)
  Beside the deeps of man's necessity
  That I may probe, in songs of love——

THALIA (*laughing*).   But I,
  Thalia, am prone to laughter, and inspire
  A golden comedy. Gods give to man
  Their greatest gift in laughter——

MELPOMENE.   Nay, in tears——

CALLIOPE. In heroism——

EUTERPE.   Beauty——

ERATO.   Nay, in love——

MUSES (*together*). Listen to me !——

90

[*The* GIRL *enters hurriedly* L. *and comes* C. *She is a modern girl, dressed for outdoors in summer. The* MUSES *turn away together in a sweeping movement expressive of frustration, bowing their heads on their arms. The* GIRL *turns impatiently to the* WRITER. *Her first words are like an echo of the* MUSES'.

GIRL. Listen to me ! . . . You promised you'd meet me at the 'bus at half-past six, and it's seven o'clock now——

[*The* WRITER *turns wearily.*

WRITER. What ? Oh, it's you——

GIRL. Me ? I should think so, indeed ! Half-past six you promised, and——

WRITER. I didn't promise. (*Rising.*) I said I couldn't . . . I said I'd like to, but that—definitely—I couldn't.

GIRL. I'm sure you as good as promised. I've been looking forward to it all day. (*Persuasively.*) Come on ! You'll be better outdoors on a nice evening like this.

WRITER. I'm sorry—but I can't, really. You know this is all the spare time I have——

GIRL. Well ?

WRITER. —and you know I'm busy——

GIRL. Busy ?

WRITER. Yes, busy—writing——

GIRL. Writing what ?

WRITER. I don't know, yet——

[*The* GIRL *looks down at the blank paper, scornfully.*

GIRL. You don't know. And you haven't even begun . . . If that's what you call busy——

WRITER. I have to get inspiration——

GIRL (*tearfully*). If *that* makes you too busy to bother about me—— (*Turns to go off* L.)

WRITER. It's the hardest part—the birth of ideas——

GIRL (*laughs scornfully.*)

WRITER. Like having a child——

GIRL (*turning at entrance L.*). You try having a child, and see the difference. (*Suddenly pleading.*) Won't you come ?

WRITER. I can't——

GIRL. It'll be lovely by the river to-night.

WRITER. I tell you I must work.

GIRL (*with disgust*). Oh, all right ! If you think so much of your silly writing . . . I daresay I shall find someone else——

> [*The* GIRL *shrugs and goes off L. The* WRITER *lights a cigarette and paces up and down stage, in difficult thought. The* MUSES *slowly turn together and look towards him. He takes no notice of them.*
>
> *The* TORMENTOR *enters R., (or rises from the floor, on which he has been stretched, with slow movements, wakening to action.) He is a demon, fantastically dressed. His movements are all eccentric. He carries, instead of the more usual poker, a gigantic quill pen, with which throughout the play he tickles or prods the* WRITER (*whose reactions are not to a prodded or tickled body, but to a troubled mind.*) *At sight of the* TORMENTOR *the* MUSES *make a concerted movement of abhorrence. He cocks a snook at them, and dogs the steps of the* WRITER, *who of course does not see him.*

TORMENTOR (*suggestively, leering over the* WRITER's *shoulder*). It will be lovely by the river to-night——

WRITER (*speaking to himself, not looking at the* TORMENTOR). I might have gone with her. I'm utterly wasting time here. I haven't got two damned ideas (*the* MUSES *express horror*) to rub together.

TORMENTOR. The green water, dappled by the leaves— and the moon-daises . . . The long, cool meadow-grass . . . Think——

WRITER. Threatened she could get someone else——

TORMENTOR. Her body is slim and young. Her kisses are sweet . . . And presently there will be dusk by the river . . . Dusk—for bats and owls—silver night-moths—and lovers——

IF IMAGINATION AMEND THEM

WRITER (*impatiently, to himself*). Oh, stop thinking of her like that, you swine ! What's the use of it ! . . . River —meadows—dusk—all temptation . . . I must work !

TORMENTOR (*springing away with derisive gestures and singing*). Cuckoo ! Cuckoo ! Cuckoo !——-

[*The* WRITER *returns to his seat. The* TORMENTOR *perches himself impudently on the desk, busily troubling the* WRITER *with his quill. The* MUSES *become gracefully tense.*

The HERO *and* HEROINE *enter R., in short, close-fitting cream tunics. They are followed by the* VILLAIN, *who wears a black tunic. The movements of the three of them are automatic, and reluctant, like those of sleepy robots. If they wear masks, the masks should be almost featureless, because they are still embryonic, waiting to be given individuality. The* VILLAIN *may express a sort of awakening villainy and stealth as he dogs the* HERO *and* HEROINE, *who could perhaps tentatively mime a love-scene as they move upstage. During this the tormented* WRITER *gnaws his pen and ruffles his hair, and the* MUSES *recite the following :*

MUSES. Born of the infinite past,
      when the light was enamoured of darkness,

    Out of the mystical dusk
      of the dawning of earliest day ;

    First revelation of Spirit, urging to godhead,

    Came Inspiration, to leaven
      the heart of our wakening clay.

    Man from his earthbound abasement
      was roused and was quickened to wonder ;

    Caught in a toil, bitter-sweet,
      of assuageless desire without name ;

    Henceforth had longing above and exceeding the
      mortal :

    Love inarticulate, drawn
      and compelled as the moth to the flame.

WRITER (*to himself*). God ! if only I could get started——

    [*The* MUSES *make gestures of urgency.*

TORMENTOR. What's the use of getting started?

[*The* MUSES *make gestures of despair.*

WRITER (*not looking at him*). I must write.

TORMENTOR. Why must you? There's nothing new to say. Everything's been said before—and better than you can say it. Everything! . . . Why don't you go out with that girl? She's beautiful!

WRITER. I must realize beauty——

TORMENTOR. Why don't you *possess* beauty?

WRITER. Oh, why do I keep thinking of her?

TORMENTOR (*maliciously*). I wonder whether she'll enjoy the other man's love?

WRITER (*reacting violently*). False love! . . . She would be false! . . . Cressida was false—and Helen——

[*Sudden enthusiasm has crept into his voice. The* MUSES *become expectant. The* HERO, HEROINE, *and* VILLAIN *brighten, and move to the chest, waiting.*

Helen! . . . Why not write about the Greeks?

[*The* MUSES *are eager to help.*

TORMENTOR. Why not? . . . On the other hand—why?

WRITER. Helen——

TORMENTOR. A taking piece—if a thought immoral. But from immoral she's become immortal . . . Love the flesh, not the imagination——

WRITER. Helen, and Paris——

[*The* HERO *and* HEROINE *open the property chest and look into it.*

All the glory of the siege of Troy . . . Yes, why shouldn't I write about the siege of Troy?

[*If the* HERO, HEROINE *and* VILLAIN *are wearing feature-less masks, they remove them, placing them in the chest. The* HERO *takes from the chest a Grecian helmet, perhaps also a cloak and sword. The* HEROINE *takes a loose Grecian dress which she slips on over her tunic. The* VILLAIN *stands for a while with his back to the audience. All the movements are suggestive of dancing. During this the* MUSES *speak as follows :*

MUSES. O godlike Paris !—Paris of Troy !—you who were wed to Oenone ;
Why did you turn from your love to the fatal arms of Helen ? . . .

EUTERPE. Here is a tale of beauty——

ERATO. A tale of the beauty of love—the hot beauty of love——

EUTERPE. No—the cold beauty of Helen. Helen who was lovelier than womankind——

CALLIOPE. Helen who inspired the noblest arms of Greece to launch their spears toward Troy. A tale, indeed, of deeds heroical——

ERATO. But deeds inspired by love——

THALIA. Oh, there was laughter, too, when all the merry generals were together, and the wine brimmed and sank in the cups. 'Twas a good comedy—all for one woman —great, foolish lives wasted ; ten years of fighting, with even the gods at loggerheads ; a noble city burned, and—*(laughing)* no more than a wooden horse to crown all——

MELPOMENE. There is more than that to the tale of Helen. It is a mighty tragedy—the tragedy of princes among men fighting and wasting their lives, in pursuit of a beauty understood not——

EUTERPE. The beauty of Helen——

ERATO. The love of Helen——

MELPOMENE. Rather say—a reaching after beauty forever beyond them, known in their souls to be higher, yet fixed in their minds upon Helen.

MUSES. O glorious Helen !—Helen the golden !—what was your grey disillusion
When from the ashes of Troy you fared again to Menelaus ?

IF IMAGINATION AMEND THEM

[*The* HERO *and* HEROINE *are now ready, and come
downstage C. as Paris and Helen. The* MUSES *group themselves as an attentive audience. The* WRITER *begins to write,
the* TORMENTOR *watching him sardonically. The following
brief sketch is done rapidly and with exaggeration of tone and
movement.*

HEROINE (*passionately*). Paris, my lover, let the city fall ;
    Our love they cannot shake—and love is all.

HERO (*sulkily*). So speaks a woman——

HEROINE.   So may a man regret
    What he so dear has prized ; and so forget
    What great occasions we have known——

HERO (*bitterly*).   Ay, great
    As any misbegotten jest of fate :
    A raging husband, a deserted wife,
    A world chaotic in unmeaning strife ;
    Friends' grief, foes' mockery, a city's pain,
    An old man's agony—and where's the gain
    To match it ?——

HEROINE (*coquettishly*). Match ? Why, but a single kiss
    Of Helen's . . . Have I stinted them ?

HERO.   Is this
    More of your woman's witchery ?

HEROINE.   Ah, no !——

HERO. Why did I leave my mountain-wife to go
    Adventuring down the wastes of love with you ?
    Ah gods ! that I could make my choice anew
    Betwixt the three immortals——

HEROINE (*tensely*).   If you could,
    Would you choose otherwise than love ?

HERO (*grimly*).   I should.

[*During the above, the* VILLAIN *has been rummaging in the
chest, and has found a Grecian helmet for himself, and a great
black bow with an arrow. He fits the arrow and draws the
bow, pointing it at the* HERO.

HEROINE (*weeping*). O false and cruel ! what have I done
    for this ?

HERO. Murdered my honour with a poisonous kiss.

[*The* HEROINE *sees the* VILLAIN, *and starts in alarm, pointing.*

HEROINE. Look, Paris !——

HERO (*carelessly, to the* VILLAIN). Why, if you'll drive out my breath
  On that dark shaft, I'll thank you for my death.

[*The* VILLAIN *laughs hugely and drops his bow and arrow back into the chest, from which he takes a child's wooden horse on wheels, which he leads downstage.*

VILLAIN. Look upon this and fear it—not my bow.

[*The* HERO *and* HEROINE *stare in bewilderment. The* WRITER *makes a gesture of despair. The* TORMENTOR *laughs, prods the* WRITER, *and waves the* HERO, HEROINE *and* VILLAIN *upstage with a large gesture.*

TORMENTOR. Frail dust of thought—back to the dust you go !

[*The* HERO, HEROINE *and* VILLAIN *replace their properties in the chest, and remain standing near it in formal poses. The* MUSES *turn away, dejectedly covering their faces. The* WRITER *tears up the sheets on which he has been working, and drops them into the waste-paper basket.*

WRITER (*disgustedly*). What a ghastly mess !

TORMENTOR (*chuckling*). Not original, either. And think how much better Homer did it.

WRITER. It seems that everything one thinks of has been done before——

TORMENTOR. And always by someone better than one-self——

WRITER. What shall I do !——

TORMENTOR. Go out and love that girl——

WRITER. I must write !

TORMENTOR. You must live.

WRITER. I am going to write !

[*The* MUSES *brighten a little.*

TORMENTOR. And, when you have finished writing, do you know what the end of it will be?

WRITER (*desperately*). Why must I be bothered with doubts?

TORMENTOR (*tickling the* WRITER). I will show you the end of it.

[*The* WRITER *gets up wearily and paces across the stage and back. The* TORMENTOR *goes upstage and claps his hands.* FRUSTRATION *enters L. He is dressed either as a fantastic postman with a bag, or as Mercury with a postman's coat and bag. His movements are fantastic, long, slow-motion, flying steps. His handling of his letters is exaggerated. The* TORMENTOR *directs his movements with his quill. The* WRITER, *who is now standing L., looking down sadly at his desk, is not aware of his presence until the* TORMENTOR *commands:*

O Spirit of Frustration, be visible to him!

[*The* TORMENTOR *chuckles.* FRUSTRATION *moves to the* WRITER *and taps him on the shoulder.*

WRITER. What—who are you?

FRUSTRATION. I am a bearer of evil tidings.

WRITER. Bear them somewhere else, then. I don't want them.

FRUSTRATION. You have brought them upon yourself.

[FRUSTRATION *takes an outsize envelope from his bag, and hands it to the* WRITER, *who tears it open and takes out a very large sheet of paper, from which he reads aloud,* FRUSTRATION *meanwhile moving round the stage with his eccentric steps, the* TORMENTOR *expressing delight, the* MUSES *dejected, and the others standing quite still.*

WRITER (*disgustedly*). Messrs. Smith, Jones and Robinson present their compliments and thank you for letting them see your manuscript entitled " Blah ! " They regret, however, that they are unable to make any offer regarding publication, and are therefore returning the manuscript under—Oh, damn !——

[*The* WRITER *savagely tears up the letter and throws it into the waste-paper basket. The* TORMENTOR *laughs, and the* MUSES *cover their faces.*

TORMENTOR (*singing*). Cuckoo ! Cuckoo ! Cuckoo !——

[*By this time* FRUSTRATION *is back at the* WRITER'S *elbow, handing another outsize envelope. Business as before.*

WRITER. Messrs. Brown, Brown, Brown and Brown are returning under separate cover your manuscript entitled " Blah ! " with their regrets that they are unable to——

TORMENTOR. Cuckoo !——

[*The* WRITER *again tears up the letter.* FRUSTRATION *comes again to his elbow, but this time, just as he is handing over a third letter, he suddenly draws it back.*

FRUSTRATION. Tuppence to pay ?

WRITER. Oh, go to Hell !

FRUSTRATION. But that's not on my round. Besides, I've more letters to deliver to you.

WRITER. How many ?

FRUSTRATION. Forty-nine.

TORMENTOR (*chuckling*). And all the same—all rejections ! . . . Cuckoo !——

WRITER (*to* FRUSTRATION). Get out !

FRUSTRATION. Tuppence to pay !

[*The* WRITER *runs at him and angrily drives him off L. Then the* WRITER *dejectedly returns to his seat.*

WRITER. If I could get inspiration——

[*The* MUSES *move to form a defensive group before the throne of* INSPIRATION.

MUSES. If you desire to possess her, speed you your art to her wooing.

[*The* TORMENTOR *comes downstage again.*

TORMENTOR. Don't take any notice of them. You'll never be able to write.

WRITER. I will write !

TORMENTOR. Think of the thousands who try, and fail . . . Publishers issue ninety-nine rejection slips for every acceptance . . . Go out after that girl!

WRITER. Why can't I get her out of my mind?

MELPOMENE. We must be urgent to help him. (*Holding out her arms towards the* WRITER'S *back.*) Think—oh, think! . . . There are great themes of tragedy——

TORMENTOR. Yes, but they are mostly Historical, and therefore mostly lies. And, anyway, they're not original——

MELPOMENE (*angrily, to the* TORMENTOR). Be quiet! No situation is original——

[*The* TORMENTOR *bows to her.*

TORMENTOR. Just what I've been telling you all——

MELPOMENE. You pay too much attention to originality of plot. Originality of *treatment* is what matters—divine inspiration to develop characters that will live——

TORMENTOR. Divine fiddlesticks to make sounds on an empty drum.

WRITER (*suddenly*). Ah, yes—perhaps—Egypt!——

[*The* WRITER *begins to write again. The* MUSES *become interested. So do the* HERO, HEROINE *and* VILLAIN.

TORMENTOR. He's at it again——

[*The* TORMENTOR *goes to the* WRITER *and looks over his shoulder, then prods him with the quill.*

Here I say, you know—what about Bill Shakespeare, to say nothing of George Bernard Shaw?

[*The* HEROINE *and* VILLAIN *are searching in the chest. The* HEROINE *takes out Cleopatra's vulture head-dress and some jewellery, including earrings of large pearls, and perhaps an Egyptian girdle, and puts them on. The* VILLAIN *takes out a festive robe, and a garland of roses for his head. He assumes these, then takes out a great wine-cup of gilded wood and a coloured balloon on a string. During these preparations, the* MUSES *speak as follows :*

MUSES. Daughter of Greece, but Queen of an older land
    Queen of old Egypt. Often your tale is told,
And oft shall be, while men have the power of love.

ERATO. So great a tale of love that men shall never know
a greater ; of a world lost by lovers for their love——

THALIA. Ay ! Lovers who could laugh, and jest, and live
inimitably——

EUTERPE. But more than that—of beauty ; of the beauty
of Cleopatra the Great, Isis-Aphrodite incarnate ; of the
beauty of Mark Antony, king among men——

CALLIOPE. Still more—of over-shadowing greatness ; the
spirit of mighty Cæsar, who gave the Queen of Egypt a
son to sit on the throne of all the world, and set the seal
of greatness upon her heart.

MELPOMENE. That is not all. Their love, and beauty,
and greatness of purpose are but notes in the swelling and
awful music of a song meet for the gods.

ERATO. Love——

THALIA. Laughter——

EUTERPE. Beauty——

CALLIOPE. An epic theme——

MELPOMENE. A tragic theme. A theme to move the
high gods to pity, and men to the terror of what the gods
ordain, that gods and men alike be purified.

MUSES. Vulture-crowned ! Goddess and queen ! Mistress
of men !
    Ruling the rulers of earth ; living and laughing at
    life !
    Setting your life on a hazard ; losing—and laughing
    at death.

[*The* HEROINE *and* VILLAIN *link arms and dance riotously
downstage, laughing, carrying the golden cup between them.
The* HERO, *who has for a time remained still with his back to
the audience, has then taken from the chest a gilded circlet of
bays for his head, and a Roman patrician's purple-bordered
toga, which he puts on. He moves downstage with attempted
majesty, which is spoilt in effect by his frequent drunken staggers.*

Meanwhile the HEROINE *smiles coquettishly at the* VILLAIN, *takes off one of her pearl earrings, and drops it into the wine-cup. While the pearl is supposed to dissolve, they kiss, the cup stretched out between one hand of each and towards the audience. Then both drink. By this time the* HERO *is downstage to R. of them, glaring angrily. They laugh at him.*

VILLAIN. A priceless wine, indeed! With a king's ransom
　　To flavour it——

HERO (*furiously*). 　　　　　　And then a queen's false lips
　　To give it venom——

HEROINE (*coolly*). 　　　　　　Antony calls me false?
　　Where then's the truth of Antony?——

HERO. 　　　　　　　　　　　　　　This fellow,
　　Who dares his lechery to flaunt with Egypt
　　Under the very nose of Antony,
　　Who is he?——

HEROINE (*laughing*). 　　Why, *you* know him well enough.

HERO. Till now I've ne'er laid eyes on him——

HEROINE. 　　　　　　　　　　　　He's known
　　To both of us—and well——

HERO. 　　　　　　　　　I know him not!——

[*To the* VILLAIN.

　　Get you away from her, or, by the gods!
　　I'll split you——

(*Feeling for his sword and not finding it.*)

　　　　　　　　　　　　　Where's my sword!——

VILLAIN (*laughing hugely*). 　　　　The sword of Antony
　　Has melted in the love of Cleopatra.

[*The* HERO *moves angrily towards the* VILLAIN.

HERO. Tell me your name——

VILLAIN. 　　　　　　　I am your other self . . .
　　Antony's folly . . . I have thrown your world
　　Your honour, and your soldier's reputation
　　Into a woman's lap——

[*The* HERO *starts, then pauses, shamed.*

HERO.   Ay, that I've done ;

I—the world's master—subject to a mistress——

[*The* HERO *covers his face with his hands. The* HEROINE
leaves the VILLAIN *and goes to him.*

HEROINE (*sweetly*).   But what a mistress !   Is this world of
          yours,
     So thrown away, too much to pay for me ?

HERO (*savagely, repulsing her*).
     If I could break these dark Egyptian bonds,
     Quench all the wild enchantment of your eyes,
     Cut loose the circlet of your wanton arms,
     I'd tell you——

HEROINE (*in mock surprise*).   What ?   My Antony grown
          cold ?

HERO (*bitterly*).   I'd be as cold as young Octavius
     Who coldly marches now against our peace. . . .
     You'll have no will of *him* when Antony
     Is by your treachery broken——

HEROINE (*amazed and angry*).   Treachery ?
     What is this word you dare to fling a queen ? . . .
     It seems my time has come to die——

HERO.   To die !
     Leave that to me.   Death is my all.   The rest
     You and your gypsy wiles have stolen from me.

[*The* VILLAIN *has been watching with amusement.*

VILLAIN.   All men are fools, but few are fools as great
          As Antony——

[*Holding out the balloon between his hands.*

                         See—here's your world that was,
     And now 'tis——

[*The* VILLAIN *chuckles and bursts the balloon under the*
HERO'S *nose. The* HERO *starts, drops to his knees, and
covers his face with his hands.*

                              nothing——

HERO.   Egypt, thus for you
>   Antony dies. (*Shouting*). Bring me a sword—a
>   sword.
>   That I may fall upon it——

> [*The* VILLAIN *laughs. The* HEROINE *hovers tensely
> between him and the* HERO. *The* WRITER *moves impatiently,
> tearing up several more sheets and dropping them into the waste-
> paper basket. The* TORMENTOR *waves the* HERO, HEROINE,
> *and* VILLAIN *upstage.*

TORMENTOR.   Get you away !——

WRITER (*groaning*). Oh lord, this is all wrong !——

> [*The* WRITER *sits holding his head in his hands. The*
> HERO, HEROINE *and* VILLAIN *replace their properties in the
> chest, and remain near it as before. The* MUSES *are all
> dejected.*

TORMENTOR. Of course it's all wrong. Who are you to
write about such things ? Besides, as I keep telling you,
it's been done before.

ERATO (*sobbing*). Oh dear ! And we came all the way
from Parnassus—for this !——

THALIA. And the air is so crowded, nowadays.

EUTERPE. The man seems to have some vague idea of
beauty——

CALLIOPE. But he'll never dig it out of the rubbish with
which his circumstances have choked his mind.

MELPOMENE. I still have hope of him . . . if he could
suffer, he could write great things.

TORMENTOR (*impudently, to the* MUSES). What a silly lot
of girls you are ! Why don't you go away, and leave
him to his commonplace job ?

MELPOMENE. Genius springs so often from the commonplace.

TORMENTOR. So you defy me ?

MELPOMENE. Don't flatter yourself so far. We scorn you.

TORMENTOR. Very well then ! You just wait and see
what I'm going to do now.

[*The* TORMENTOR *strikes a melodramatic attitude and stalks largely upstage. The* MUSES *make a concerted gesture of apprehension. The* TORMENTOR *claps his hands.* NECESSITY *enters L. He is dressed as a fantastic policeman. A sheaf of blue summonses is stuck through his belt. His movements are all exaggerated.*

THALIA. Why, it's only a policeman !——

CALLIOPE. A mere policeman !——

NECESSITY. A mere policeman, indeed ! I'll have you know, young woman, that the police are never *mere*. They are of the utmost importance——

EUTERPE. In what way ?

NECESSITY. They—well, they control the traffic.

[NECESSITY *strikes an attitude and mimes traffic control, waving, beckoning, forbidding, and occasionally " honk-honking " in a raucous voice. The* WRITER, *of course, does not know he is there, and remains looking dejectedly at his blank paper.*

THALIA (*to* NECESSITY). Why don't you learn to dance gracefully ?

TORMENTOR (*to* NECESSITY). Take no notice of them. I've got a job for you——

[NECESSITY *salutes and comes downstage C. The* TORMENTOR *sits on the* WRITER'S *desk, prodding him.* I'm still warning you. Better give up.

WRITER. I'll keep on—if I do get dozens of rejections. In time they may become acceptances——

TORMENTOR. Even if any of your trash ever is accepted, you'll never be able to make a living as a writer. Think of the number of them at it ! . . . You'll live poorly and dangerously on next door to nothing . . . You'll never be able to pay your bills, and your creditors will have you in the County Court.

WRITER. Thoughts of poverty aren't going to frighten me off——

TORMENTOR. Spirit of Necessity! Be visible to him!

[NECESSITY *salutes again and moves behind the* WRITER, *taking from his pocket an outsize police whistle, which he blows in the* WRITER's *ear. The* WRITER *reacts violently.*

WRITER. Who the hell are you?

NECESSITY (*exaggeratedly grim*). I am the Mother of Invention, and I know no Law.

WRITER. What?

NECESSITY. I am Necessity!

WRITER. Necessity for what?

NECESSITY. Nothing! Just Necessity.

WRITER. Well, you aren't necessary to me. Go away!

NECESSITY. Are you Mr. Wouldbe Writer?

WRITER. I am.

NECESSITY. Ah! then I've got something for you——

WRITER. What?

NECESSITY. An invitation.

WRITER. An invitation? To a party?

NECESSITY. Not exactly to a party. But it's a very pressing invitation.

[NECESSITY *hands a summons to the* WRITER.

You are hereby invited to Court. All the County will be there.

WRITER. But—this is a summons——

NECESSITY. Exactly.

[NECESSITY *cuts capers and recites :*

He who will not pay his debts
Such a summons quickly gets ;
Should he obdurate remain
Someone surely will distrain ;
Spoil the child and spare the rod,
And book another room in quod.

WRITER. Go away! I don't like you!

[*The* WRITER *disgustedly throws the summons into the waste-paper basket.*

What will they do if I don't?

NECESSITY. Don't what?

WRITER. Don't pay.

[NECESSITY *approaches the* WRITER *tensely, on tiptoe, and bending to his ear, says in an exaggeratedly cautious, loud whisper:*

NECESSITY. Send the Broker's Man.

WRITER. Send the broker's man because I'm broke?

NECESSITY. Precisely.

[*He presents another summons. The* WRITER *jumps up in sudden excitement, holding the summons in his hand.*

WRITER. The broker's man! You've given me an idea . . . (*Gives back the summons to* NECESSITY.) Here you are! Here's something for yourself! Now be off!——

[NECESSITY *takes the summons and gazes at it, scratching his head. The* WRITER *runs him off L. The* TORMENTOR *makes gestures of despair.*

TORMENTOR. Am I to go on tormenting this fellow all night?

WRITER. An idea! What an idea!——

[*The* WRITER *returns to his seat, and begins to write feverishly. The* MUSES, HERO, HEROINE *and* VILLAIN *wake to renewed interest. The* TORMENTOR *and the* MUSES *group themselves about the* WRITER'S *desk, watching him. After an instant, however,* MELPOMENE, CALLIOPE, EUTERPE, *and* ERATO *move disgustedly away and group themselves in dejected defence of* INSPIRATION. THALIA, *laughing softly, points over the* WRITER'S *shoulder, eagerly directing him. The* TORMENTOR *tickles the* WRITER *with his quill, then tries to tickle* THALIA.

THALIA. That will do! We haven't been introduced, and I was properly brought up, anyway.

TORMENTOR. What a pity !——

THALIA. That we haven't been introduced ?

TORMENTOR. That you were properly brought up.

[THALIA *smacks the* TORMENTOR'S *face. He laughs, and concentrates on the* WRITER.

You know, all this is very silly. Besides, it's been done by—oh, lots of people !—and better than you're doing it.

WRITER. I won't have any doubts ! I will go on with it !——

THALIA (*forgetting herself in her enthusiasm*). Attaboy !——

[*The other* MUSES *express concerted disgust.*

TORMENTOR (*to* THALIA). They'll kick you out of Helicon for that.

[THALIA *ignores the* TORMENTOR, *encouraging the* WRITER. *During the above the* HEROINE *and* VILLAIN *have again been taking properties from the chest, the* HERO *standing stiffly with his back to the audience. The* HEROINE *now has on a modern, wicked little hat with a short veil, the* VILLAIN *has a butler's tail coat, with a collar, shirtfront, and bow. The* VILLAIN *(as a typical stage butler) comes pompously downstage with two light chairs (he may get them from offstage), which he makes a great show of arranging with accuracy. He then retires upstage and the* HEROINE *comes downstage and sits on one of the chairs, making herself up in mime.*

HEROINE (*continuing to look into an imaginary glass, and to use an imaginary lipstick*). Oh, Gustave !——

VILLAIN (*moving downstage*). My name, milady, is 'Erbert.

HEROINE. I prefer to call you Gustave. So much more—er—devastating . . . Gustave, do you think I ought to wear this hat indoors, in my own house ?

VILLAIN (*coughing*). Scarcely your own 'ouse, milady.

HEROINE. Oh, of course ! I was forgetting. The instalments haven't been paid, have they ?

VILLAIN. No, milady. The hinstalments upon nothing 'ave been paid. (*Sadly.*) Not even upon me.

HEROINE. Oh, dear ! How too, too—er—too——

VILLAIN. Exactly ! I expect to be collected at any moment.

HEROINE. What a nuisance for you—I mean, for me . . . But I was asking your advice, Gustave. Ought I to wear this hat ?

VILLAIN. No, milady.

HEROINE. Why not ?

VILLAIN. Because it isn't yours.

HEROINE. Don't be silly ! I'm talking social etiquette—not morals.

VILLAIN. I see ! That does make a difference, doesn't it ? . . . Well, if you don't wear anythink helse with a dress like that (*indicating her tunic*) how's them (*indicating the audience*) to know what period you're supposed to be of—er, from—er, of ?——

HEROINE. Precisely—I mean, quite ! Serve the tea, Gustave !

VILLAIN. Beg pardon, milady, but there's a broker's man coming this afternoon——

HEROINE (*indignantly*). A broker's *man* ! Why not the broker himself ?

VILLAIN. I think it's more usual for them, milady, to send their men. You see, milady, since you won't pay the hinstalments on the furniture——

HEROINE. Can't——

VILLAIN. Can't or won't, it's all the same to them.

HEROINE. What dreadfully indiscriminating creatures . . . The tea, Gustave !——

VILLAIN. Very good, milady . . . Er—suppose the—er—person comes ?

HEROINE. Entertain him in the servants' hall.

VILLAIN (*bowing*). Yes, milady.

[*The* VILLAIN *goes upstage, to return almost immediately, holding up his hands as though bearing a tea-tray, and arranging this upon an imaginary table, giving little dabs of finishing touches. During the foregoing the* HERO *has taken from the chest a top-hat, monocle, and gold-knobbed cane, and assumed them. He now mimes pressing a bell, and assumes an attitude of waiting at a front door.*

HEROINE. That is the bell, Gustave. The—er—broker's representative, perhaps.

VILLAIN. Oh no, your ladyship ! Such persons always use the tradesmen's entrance.

[*The* VILLAIN *goes upstage. He mimes opening the front door. There is a moment's further miming between him and the* HERO, *then the* HERO *solemnly hands him the hat and cane, which he solemnly puts on the chest. He then moves ponderously downstage, followed by the* HERO, *steps to one side, and announces.*

Lord Pneuly-Poore.

[*The* HERO *comes downstage and shakes hands with the* HEROINE, *who immediately languishes with exaggeration. The* VILLAIN *returns upstage and stands there with his back to the audience.*

HEROINE. Do I know you ?

HERO. I don't think so.

HEROINE. Ought I to ?

HERO. Well—I'm not considered very respectable——

HEROINE. How too sweet ! Then I certainly ought to know you ! I think respectability is so much more important to the *lower* classes, don't you ?

HERO. Of course.

HEROINE. Will you take tea ?

HERO. Naturally. I take anything.

[*The* HEROINE *mimes pouring out.*

HEROINE. How many lumps ?

HERO. Seventeen.

[*The* HEROINE *starts.*

Sorry ! I was thinking of your age.

HEROINE (*pleased*).   Oh, how too *utter* !   And how dear of you to come and see me.

[*The* HERO *mimes taking a sandwich and speaking with his mouth full.*

HERO.   I had to come.

HEROINE (*melting*).   Had to ?   Why ?

HERO.   Because of you, of course.

HEROINE (*nearly melting into his arms*).   Because of me ?   How adorable !

HERO.   Because of you !   How deplorable !

[*The* HEROINE *starts back.*

You won't pay your instalments, and I have to make a living somehow.   I'm the——

[*Probably it will be more effective not to include the words " broker's man," but please yourselves. Anyway, there is an immediate and very loud gong, off. The* HEROINE *and* HERO *spring up, and run rapidly upstage, taking their chairs with them. They, with the* VILLAIN, *replace their properties in the chest, and resume their statuesque poses.*

TORMENTOR (*as they go*).   And about time, too !

THALIA (*disgustedly, to the* WRITER).   Do you call that comedy ?

[*Thalia goes R. to the other* MUSES. *The* WRITER *tears up his sheets, throws them in the waste-paper basket, rises, and paces about, tearing his hair. The* TORMENTOR *follows him with mocking gestures, which, however, he abandons after a moment in favour of more serious attempts at dissuasion.*

TORMENTOR.   You've still time to catch that girl before she catches anyone else . . . Don't be a fool !   (*Angrily.*)   Would you be like Prometheus—chained by your ambition to a rock of perpetual torture ; devoured by regrets for what you have thrown away ?

WRITER (*pacing feverishly*).   I *will* go on writing ! . . . But what ?——

[*The* TORMENTOR *shrugs his shoulders, taps his forehead at the audience, significantly, and claps his hands. The* WRITER *is now standing still, facing downstage.* PROPAGANDA *enters R. He is dressed as a workman, and carries a hammer and sickle. He speaks to the* WRITER, *who does not see him, but looks straight at the audience, and speaks as if answering his own thoughts. During the earlier part of* PROPAGANDA'S *appearance, if desired, the* VILLAIN *may take from the chest a red flag, with which he, the* HERO *and the* HEROINE, *march to and fro across the back of the stage. The* MUSES *express an unwilling interest.*

HERO, HEROINE and VILLAIN (*together, mechanically*). Left! Left! Write of the Left! Write of the Left!

PROPAGANDA (*scornfully*). You dare to waste time wondering what to write about, when your pen is needed to help the crushed millions of the starving poor!

WRITER. I don't understand politics and economics——

PROPAGANDA. Then you should. Politics and economics enter into everything.

WRITER. It's all so sordid—so unbeautiful.

PROPAGANDA (*letting himself go*). Millions of men out of work—millions of children starving—millions of lives deliberately ground into the mud by a thieving state; a lying, hypocritical Church; a selfish, grasping Capitalism . . . The whole world is rotten nationally and internationally. To keep a morally lousy minority in luxurious lechery——

[*The* MUSES *recoil and cover their ears with their hands in horror. The* TORMENTOR *laughs silently. The* WRITER *looks bewildered.*

—we must constantly be plunged into the 'orrors—horrors—of war.

WRITER. Why does one have to think of war—unemployment—sordid fear——

PROPAGANDA (*disgustedly*). And you, with a pen and a brain and the will to write, are wondering what to write about——

IF IMAGINATION AMEND THEM

[SENTIMENTALITY *enters diffidently L., peering about her, and trips downstage to the* WRITER. *She is a maiden lady of romantic disposition, possibly in a lavender-coloured dress of the Mid- or Late-Victorian period. As she speaks into the* WRITER'S *left ear,* PROPAGANDA *goes upstage and changes his workman's coat and cap for the tail coat and top-hat worn by the* VILLAIN *and* HERO *in the previous scene. The hammer, sickle, and red flag are put into the chest, together with the coat and cap.*

SENTIMENTALITY (*gushingly*). I think it such a pity that writers nowadays so seldom write sweet love stories like they used to write. I do so adore a nice romance in which virtue triumphs over vice—vice must be only vaguely suggested, of course——

[*By this time the* MUSES, *except* ERATO, *have all turned their backs in disgust. The* HERO, HEROINE *and* VILLAIN, *upstage, might be sketchily miming saccharine melodrama.* PROPAGANDA, *if he is dressed, is standing pompously as though about to address his constituents.*

—and where there are (*clasping ecstatic hands to her stomach*) happy wedding-bells on the last page.

[ERATO *shrugs and turns her back, joining her sisters in disgust.*

I do so love a happy ending, don't you ?

WRITER (*to himself*). Easy enough to sell sentimental twaddle, but who wants to write that ?

SENTIMENTALITY. All the members of my Women's Institute, and the Mothers' Bright Hour, love happy endings. And the dear Vicar does. They like their heroines to be pure——

[PROPAGANDA *comes downstage, clearing his throat. He moves prosperously to R. of the* WRITER. SENTIMENTALITY *looks frightened and stops speaking. The* HERO, HEROINE, *and* VILLAIN *stand to attention in a row.*

HERO, HEROINE and VILLAIN (*together, mechanically*). Right ! Right ! Write of the Right ! Write of the Right !

Propaganda (*unctuously, to the* Writer). You know, my boy, you've a great responsibility. As I was saying the other day, when I gave away the prizes at my Old School —it's up to the youngsters of to-day to preserve our ideals, to be clean and manly, to set their shoulders to the wheel, and play a straight bat, and keep the Old Tie flying— above all, to preserve the Old Country from the mildew of Communism and the dry-rot of Pacifism . . . When I was a boy, my boy, we weren't afraid of war—war makes men manly—and we didn't have all these silly ideas about giving the dole and things to the lower classes. Our forefathers—who built the Old Empire, our glorious trust—didn't worry about the lower classes. Why should we?

[*During the above speech the* Hero, Heroine *and* Villain *mechanically and quietly interject* " Hear, · hear ! "

Writer. Everything gets so mixed——

[*The* Muses *have turned together, and are gazing in astonishment and dismay at this new specimen of propaganda. The* Writer *is staring at the audience, troubled. The* Tormentor *moves C. and touches* Sentimentality *and* Propaganda *with his quill. Then he tickles the* Writer, *who starts.*

Tormentor. Sentimentality—Propaganda—I command you to be visible to him.

[Sentimentality *and* Propaganda *grip the* Writer's *arms, and begin to talk very rapidly, one against the other. Their lips move continuously, so that each appears to be speaking all the time, but audible only intermittently.* Propaganda's *voice changes where possible as he changes his sentiments. He might also remove his top-hat every time he is " Left." The* Writer *looks from one to the other in bewilderment. Soon he is holding his ears against both. The* Hero, Heroine *and* Villain *may sway in emphasis of the rhythm.*

Sentimentality. If your tales are really pure——

Propaganda. They grind the faces of the poor——

Sentimentality. Heroines with eyes of blue——

Propaganda. Yellow-livered blacklegs, too——

SENTIMENTALITY.   Pave the way to sweet content——

PROPAGANDA.   Build a mighty armament——

SENTIMENTALITY.   Wedding-bells that lovers bless——

PROPAGANDA.   Tell of war and manliness——

SENTIMENTALITY.   Lovers' eyes, enchanted sparks——

PROPAGANDA.   Read the writings of Karl Marx——

SENTIMENTALITY.   Lips as ripe as sugar-plums——

PROPAGANDA.   Rotting in the stinking slums——

SENTIMENTALITY.   Little hands, as lilies white——

PROPAGANDA.   Take the sword, and aid the *Right*——

SENTIMENTALITY.   Tender looks that mutely plead——

PROPAGANDA.   Never heed the workers' need——

SENTIMENTALITY.   Anguished heart, of love bereft——

PROPAGANDA.   Beat 'em up, and help the *Left*——

SENTIMENTALITY.   Bells amid the evening shades——

PROPAGANDA.   Bombs across the barricades——

SENTIMENTALITY.   Lily maid, with crystal soul——

PROPAGANDA.   Lazy-rotten, on the Dole——

SENTIMENTALITY.   Gentle echoes where she trod——

PROPAGANDA.   Might is Right, and Mammon, God !

[*Both are by this time shouting at the* WRITER. *He makes a great effort, shakes them off, and stands downstage C., shivering with fear.*

TORMENTOR.   This has gone on long enough.

[*The* TORMENTOR *claps his hands again.* FRUSTRATION *and* NECESSITY *enter L., with grimly eccentric movements.* SENTIMENTALITY *and* PROPAGANDA *back upstage a few paces. The* HERO, HEROINE *and* VILLAIN *come downstage, and, with the* TORMENTOR, *they all form a semicircle about the* WRITER. *The* MUSES *are huddled about the throne of* INSPIRATION, *dejectedly, their faces averted.*

The eight in the semicircle advance upon and retreat from the WRITER *in nightmare fashion, rather like a dance of witch-doctors. As they do so they repeat in grimly monotonous*

fashion. " Blah, blah—*blah !* . . . Blah blah—*blah !* "
(*Drums offstage could intensify this effect.*) *The* WRITER *has
swung round upon them, his back to the audience, his arms
spread wide in fear. If possible the light has dimmed and
changed, with a spot on the* WRITER, *and many shadows. The
dancers gradually quicken their rhythm. The* WRITER *runs
vainly from side to side of the semicircle, then drops on his
knees C., bowing his head on his arms. All except the* TOR-
MENTOR *stand still, pointing at him. The* TORMENTOR *steps
forward and stands over him, the quill raised in both hands
like a spear that he is about to plunge downwards into him.
There is a brief, tense pause. Then the* WRITER *looks up,
in agony.*

WRITER (*desperately*). Let me go ! Would you impale me
on my own pen ? Haven't I suffered enough ?

HERO. He has not suffered enough to give us life.

HEROINE. We have not yet lived through him.

VILLAIN. Therefore he must suffer more, or we must
go back to oblivion.

TORMENTOR (*dramatically, to the* WRITER).

If you persist in this your mad ambition,
You must achieve it through your agony.

FRUSTRATION. I shall be ever at your elbow with the
Cup of Tantalus.

NECESSITY. And I, to paint your difficulties blacker.

PROPAGANDA. And I, to drive you many ways at once.

SENTIMENTALITY. And I, to drag you from the highest
level of your art.

WRITER (*shouting, desperately*). Inspiration ! Goddess and
woman ! Hear me !

[*The Writer, still on his knees, holds up his arms (not
looking towards* INSPIRATION). *The* TORMENTOR *and the
others shrink back a pace, with a concerted hiss of frustrated
malice. The* MUSES *revive a little, but still remain grouped
defensively about* INSPIRATION. *The* TORMENTOR *lowers
his quill. The* WRITER *begins to speak gently, but his voice
rises in a crescendo of power.*

> I was a humble votary of thine,
> Full of the sense of my unworthiness ;
> But I must dare so greatly as to aspire
> To thy most gracious person. Do not stoop
> From dim abodes of ecstasy to give
> Gentle forgiveness . . . Great is my presumption
> And I'll have nothing pitiful of thee——

[*The* WRITER *springs to his feet, sweeping the* TORMENTOR *and his satellites back towards L. with a wide gesture. The* MUSES *completely revive, posing themselves proudly now about* INSPIRATION. *But the* WRITER *is not yet looking towards* INSPIRATION. *He continues, passionately :*

> I'll have thy love, thyself !——
> Kneeling, I win thee ; worshipping, possess
> As man to woman, now I know my power
> At once to supplicate and to command !——

[*The* GIRL *enters quietly L., visible, but out of the way of the others. She watches the* WRITER *in astonishment, because she sees only him. The* WRITER *drives the* TORMENTOR *and the others upstage L. with grand gestures.*

> Torments and doubts—away !——

[*The* HERO, HEROINE *and* VILLAIN *remain upstage in stiff lay-figure poses.* NECESSITY, FRUSTRATION, PROPAGANDA *and* SENTIMENTALITY *are driven off L. The* TORMENTOR *makes a last effort.*

TORMENTOR.   We shall return——

WRITER (*very grandly*).

> Return—and thus I'll scatter you again ;
> Return—and every time of your returning,
> I shall make large my power in *routing* you !——

[*The* TORMENTOR *shrinks off L., backward. The* GIRL *moves diffidently towards the* WRITER.

GIRL.   What's the matter ? Have you gone mad ? You're fighting shadows——

[*The* WRITER *ignores her. He is looking towards R., not directly at* INSPIRATION, *but as if in quest of her.*

Why do you stay here, all alone ? It's a glorious evening, outside——

[*Pause. The* WRITER *takes no notice of her.*

I had to come back . . . Don't you love me any more ?

   [*She puts her arms about the* WRITER'S *neck. He gently repulses her.*

WRITER. There is a time for everything. Now I must work.

GIRL (*suddenly angry*). If I leave you now, mind, it is for always.

WRITER (*sadly*). If you try to hinder me now, you will hinder me for always.

GIRL. But—don't you love me ?

WRITER. Yes.

GIRL. Wouldn't you rather be out there with me—by the river ?

WRITER. Yes.

GIRL. Then——

   [*Again she tries to embrace him, and is again repulsed, though sadly.*

WRITER. One day, perhaps, I shall have time for love. But now—there are other things——

GIRL. Oh-h-h——

   [*The* GIRL *turns, trying to be scornful, takes a step or two towards the entrance L., breaks into tears, runs to the* WRITER'S *chair, and sinks into it with her head on her arms, sobbing. The* WRITER *looks after her for a moment, half holds out his arms to her (the* MUSES *momentarily anxious), then pulls himself together, turns his back on her, and walks slowly to the dais, falling on his knees before the throne of* INSPIRATION.

MUSES (*reciting together*).

   Phœnix arose from his ashes
     in strength of new beauty and wonder,
  Spreading his wide wings of hope
     to the freedom of heaven again ;

So will endeavour, achieving,
　　strike darkness asunder,
Born to the joy of fulfilment
　　from out of a matrix of pain.

[Two of the Muses *gradually lift the veil from* Inspiration *who rises and walks slowly to the* Writer, *stretching out her hands to him. The* Writer *bends and kisses her hands, remaining in this position until the Curtain. The* Muses *continue:*

There is no deed of creation
　　but needs must destroy in the doing
Some of the flowers that have sprung
　　where the feet of Immortals have trod ;
Strive then, and think but of striving ;
　　no matter ensuing
Ever can break man again
　　from the part of the man that is God.

SLOW CURTAIN.

T. B. MORRIS

The White Horseman

A Play in One Act

LONDON
FREDERICK MULLER LTD.
29 Great James Street, W.C.1

FIRST PUBLISHED BY FREDERICK MULLER, LTD.
IN 1948
PRINTED IN GREAT BRITAIN BY WYMAN & SONS LTD.
LONDON, READING AND FAKENHAM

THE CHARACTERS

DEREK GARTH.
DELPHINE.
JEANNE BIDET.
SUSAN JAMES.
PHYLLIS KNIGHTS.
BERT ROBINS.
MARTHA ROBINS.
CLINT P. HAMBERGER.
MARY CLARK.
TONY.
TALBOT DRENNAN.
MARILLA DRENNAN.
VALERIE KEMPTON.
AN OLD SHEPHERD.

THE SCENE

A mountain slope in the Bernese Alps, just after dawn on a day of early October, 1937.

Backstage the ground rises to the edge of an imagined precipice, giving, as the light increases, a magnificent view of snowclad mountain peaks and sky. To R., the lowest part of the stage, are a few pine trunks. To L. the rock goes up almost vertically in a great cliff face. Entrance R., from the valley, and upstage L., by a narrow and dangerous path round a buttress of rock (up the mountain). This path is reached over a large flat rock some feet above the general level of the stage, which makes a dizzy platform upstage L. The platform is approached by lower rocks making rough steps, and is not difficult to reach, though only the strong-headed would stay long near its upstage edge, which overhangs the precipice. There are other rocks scattered about the stage. The sunrise is imagined as taking place off backstage L. The characters face in a downstage L. direction when looking up towards the peak of the mountain they are on. The light grows gradually through the play, to sunrise near the end. Distant cow-bells are heard at intervals from the valley. The characters are dressed against the morning cold.

THE WHITE HORSEMAN

Majestic music. The Curtain rises on a dim stage, as dawn has just broken. Towards L. the sky is faintly tinged with rose, and some of the distant peaks are picked out with light. DEREK GARTH, *a tall and impressive-looking man of about thirty-five, with the broad brow and calm gaze of a dreamer, is standing on the rocky platform near the backstage edge, looking out over the gulf. The music fades out.*

GARTH (*awed*). The last dawn . . .

[*He turns to face downstage.*

Far below in the valley, yet in darkness——
Night of the day, deeper night of the mind——
Men wait, and never know
And never trouble themselves to know
For what they wait ;
All over the world, in the world's valleys,
The fortunate sleeping, the others stirring, un-
 willing, from pain or necessity,
But few preparing ;
Few who have willingly struggled out of the sleep
 of the mind,
Out of the piled sloth of the ages of mankind
Into a comprehension of to-day.

[*Pause.*

Here where the air, thin and lonely, steals down
 the face of the mountain,
Clinging to night, reluctant as night for day's
 inevitability ;
Here is clean calm at last, a right sense of proportion
After the goose-flesh touch of horror over the years

And heavier horror, bolder, bolder, more immediate,
strident,
Feet resounding, clanging, the feet of doom . . .
Loud and louder, louder . . .
The wheezy clacking of the hotel clock, magnified
As the years grew out of the minutes—one night
more,
Last night—the last night . . .
And I awake, more wakeful than the prisoner
To be shot at dawn, hanged at eight ; wakeful,
alone, wondering
What may one do with the years of the minutes ?
Prayer
Is no more possible. Too late, now, for prayer.
There is impertinence in delayed repentance.
As ye have done, so shall ye come to judgment.
For good or ill the preparation is over,
The examination paper blotted and folded.
Square the shoulders and face the judge, forgetting
All weakness of excuses . . . But who could have
prayed
In such a place ? Oh dawn, blot out the memory !
The furniture, shabby, ghostly pompous yet
In the little light of the chill and laggard hours ;
The gilt paint flaking away from mirrors in which
one caught
Fugitive glimpses of that other self
One carries like an Old Man of the Sea
And strives to forget, vainly, or vainly strives to
conquer ;
That other self—how much peeps out of the eyes
to the eyes of others ?
The fly-blown mirrors know it and leer in the night
While the clock clacks to the rhythm of the in-
exorable. . . .
Do they allow a mirror to the prisoner
In the condemned cell, waiting the chaplain and
rope ?
The condemned cell—widened—as wide as the
world,

Where men and hogs and men await—alone——
Each unknowing—alone . . .

[Pause. Then he throws out his arms as if in supplication, looking up at the sky, speaking more passionately.

Oh God ! *I* know Thy purpose for to-day.
From end to end of every laggard year
Hast thou pursued me with the awful knowledge
Thyself to man forbade . . .
I have rejected it ; I have run from Thee,
And I have turned again, and covered my eyes, and groped,
Shamed, reluctant, compelled, toward that knowledge,
Toward the inexorable Now . . .

[Pause. He glances off to R., speaking to himself in a changed tone.

They are coming, the others I have drawn up here to the mountain. In fear, in curiosity—some perhaps in faith. I must have a moment longer——

[He moves off quickly round the rock upstage L. A moment later DELPHINE, *a young girl, thin, pale and poorly dressed, enters R., quickly and nervously, as though some excitement stronger than herself is driving her. She stops suddenly, disappointed.*

DELPHINE. But he is not here.

*[*JEANNE BIDET, *a simple, matter-of-fact old woman of working class, wearing a shawl and clutching a cheap crucifix, enters R.*

JEANNE. He will come. But certainly he will come. His eyes were true. I've had three husbands—they all deceived me, and not one of them had eyes like his.

DELPHINE. He said—at sunrise.

JEANNE. Ah ! I wonder how he knows ? But he is so certain. (*Comfortably.*) Father Pierre said he is wrong.

DELPHINE (*starting*). Ah—no!

JEANNE (*still easy, garrulous*). Father Pierre said that such information would be given only to the Church, and this man, this Englishman, this M'sieu' Garth, what is he? At best a heretic, at worst a heathen. (*With half-humorous confidence.*) But Father Pierre is a good soul. He understands our little weaknesses. "Jeanne Bidet," he said, "you are an old busybody and inquisitive as a child. If you must take an early walk up the mountain to satisfy your curiosity, be sure you wear a good thick shawl against the morning cold," he said, and he laughed. "If you were as fat as I," he said, "you'd keep to the valleys." (*She laughs.*)

DELPHINE. We shouldn't laugh.

JEANNE. I don't know. Myself, I've never believed the good God minds us laughing. And we've plenty of crying to do between the laughs.

[DELPHINE *has moved upstage. She looks over the precipice, drawing back with a shudder.*

DELPHINE. What a frightful drop!

JEANNE. Keep away from the edge.

DELPHINE (*another peep*). All dark and shadowy, far and far down. But why should I fear it now—or anything?

JEANNE (*going to her, clutching her arm*). Come away, or Satan will tempt you over—even now.

DELPHINE. He has often tempted me, by water at night —black and beckoning water——

JEANNE. Holy Mother!

DELPHINE. It would have been so easy to die. It has been so hard to live—so hard. (*Eagerly.*) But there's no need to fear any more, is there? It's true, isn't it? (*More urgently, as though stifling doubt.*) Isn't it?

JEANNE (*cautiously*). Fear gets twined about our roots like bindweed about roses. But we must hope—and strengthen hope with a little prayer.

DELPHINE. Why doesn't he come?

JEANNE. He will be here, little one. Patience!

DELPHINE. It's so hard to be sure—not to be afraid. They turned me out into the street yesterday.

JEANNE. Ah, cruel! And so cold!

DELPHINE. I've no money. I owe weeks of rent.

JEANNE. Poor little one! What is your name?

DELPHINE. Delphine. (*Pause.*) Oh, can I believe it? Hunger and cold and fear all gone?

JEANNE (*placidly*). At least poverty is an advantage to us now—if what he says is true. I say no more than " if "——

[SUSAN JAMES, *an Englishwoman of late middle age, enters R. She is well but plainly dressed, quiet and confident. She looks around at the view.*

SUSAN. A beautiful place. I knew he would bring us to a beautiful place.

DELPHINE. You believe him?

SUSAN. I have waited years for to-day, believing.

DELPHINE. Then——(*She breaks off, too eager to speak.*)

SUSAN. There will be no more tears, for those who have caused no tears.

JEANNE. Ah! That is beautiful! I am Madame Jeanne Bidet, a widow who has at last learned her lesson— after the third time. It consoles one to know that marriage is not necessary in Heaven. (*Indicating* DELPHINE.) This is little Delphine.

SUSAN. My name is Susan James. I am English.

JEANNE. Ah, the English! They drink tea—tea, even at this hour of the morning. But you do not like my little joke, now?

SUSAN. Why not? I think we should all be as normal as we can. The waiting is hard. This last half-hour will be hardest.

DELPHINE. I thought he would be here.

SUSAN. He will come soon.

[PHYLLIS KNIGHTS, *a fussy and faded maiden lady, carrying a prayer-book and hung about with chains and amulets, hurries on R., breathless.*

PHYLLIS. Oh dear! I've hurried so—and my heart— (*She sits on a rock.*) There! (*Rapidly.*) I thought everyone would be here before me.

SUSAN (*calmly*). Don't worry, Miss Knights. You are in good time.

PHYLLIS (*fussily arranging her chains and dress*). Positively I can't decide whether to believe him or not. I mean— well, we all know what's likely to happen—I mean, what's going to happen some time—but just fancy it happening to us! However, I said to myself : " There's no harm in going to see. Then, if nothing happens, you can return to bed for a little rest after breakfast."

SUSAN (*still calm*). You will not return for breakfast.

PHYLLIS (*starting*). Oh! That is—er—well, one can't help being startled, can one? Not that I haven't always led a very good life.

SUSAN. I've had a long time to get used to the idea.

PHYLLIS. Do you think we should perhaps sing a hymn, or something?

SUSAN. I think not, at present. The calm of the mountains is a song in itself.

PHYLLIS. Eh? Er—yes. Yes, of course. You know, I wondered whether I might not bring poor Tibby. But I thought perhaps it might be a little—er—almost irreverent, in the circumstances. So I left the poor darling asleep in her basket. (*A little fearfully.*) I hope —oh, I do hope she will not wake before it happens. One feels—oh, it's frightening——

SUSAN. There's no need to worry.

PHYLLIS. How calm you are.

SUSAN. Of course. I was one of the first he told—years ago.

PHYLLIS. And that would make a difference. Such a beautiful young man ! What a clergyman he would have made ! I met him only two days ago, at the hotel.

DELPHINE. I heard him speak at the street corner.

JEANNE. So did I. The irreverent ones down there call him John the Baptist.

PHYLLIS. I'm frightened—yet I feel I should be more frightened. After all, though one hears so much in sermons—especially the dear Vicar's sermons when I was a girl ; a solid hour always and so brimstoney— it is quite unexpected. I must say I am glad of the little warning we have had. (*Confidentially, to* SUSAN.) I took a bath last night, though Friday is my night, really. (*Settling herself more comfortably, with some satisfaction.*) So I am all ready—just in case——

[*She breaks off with a nervous little giggle. All look R. as the voices of* BERT *and* MARTHA ROBINS *are heard off. They are prosperous tradespeople of middle age and humble origin, who are on their first holiday abroad. Their dialect is merely indicated, it may be altered to North country, Cockney or any other to the Producer's wishes. If North, however, the reference to Brighton later might be altered to Blackpool.*

ROBINS (*off, loud and cheerful*). Come on, Mother ! Only just round the corner.

MARTHA (*querulously*). I'm sure if I'd known it were s' far, you 'ouldn't a-got me t' leave my bed t'——

ROBINS. 'Ere we are !

[*He enters, followed by* MARTHA, *R.*

'Mornin', everyone.

OTHERS. Good morning.

ROBINS (*very sure of himself*). Thought me an' Mrs. Robins might as well come an' see this 'ere stunt.

MARTHA (*sitting on a rock*). 'Tis a long way up. I declare I never was on such a road. If you ask me, it ain't worth the trouble. On 'oliday, too——

SUSAN (*seriously*). It is not a stunt, my friend.

ROBINS (*laughing, mopping his brow, easily*). Oh, come now, ma'am ! You surely don't believe as this is true ?

SUSAN. It is certainly true. }
DELPHINE (*anxiously*). Oh yes ! }

ROBINS. But—I ask you ! Just think, ma'am. Use y'r commonsense. I'll not say the young chap 'asn't got a way with 'im—the gift o' the gab—but (*laughing*) well, is it likely now ? 'Appen some time, o' course. But——

MARTHA (*interrupting*). Don't talk s'much, Father. You always did talk too much.

ROBINS. An' why not ? I reckon I've earned my right t' open my mouth a bit. (*To the others.*) Started wi' nothin', I did—ten years old, a mill-boy. I owns that mill, now, an' three others—an' all honest, too. No monkey business. My employees got no cause t' complain about Bert Robins.

PHYLLIS. Er—very creditable, I'm sure.

SUSAN. But not much use just now.

ROBINS. Oh ? An' why not ? Listen 'ere ma'am—an' all o' you. Me an' Mrs. Robins is enjoyin' our first 'oliday abroad. No time t' get further than Brighton afore this.

MARTHA. I'd rather 'ave Brighton.

ROBINS. Shut up, Mother ! (*To the others.*) We're improvin' ourselves. Mind you, 'tis a bit expensive. That's why I thought we shouldn't miss this 'ere bit of a do as don't cost nothin'.

SUSAN (*horrified*). Please don't talk like that—please !

[*Her urgency impresses the others for a moment, except* ROBINS, *who chuckles and goes to the edge of the precipice, looking over.*

ROBINS. Crumbs ! We're up a depth ! Come an' look 'ow far we've come up, Mother.

MARTHA. I'm stayin' 'ere.

[CLINT P. HAMBERGER, *a film producer, large, brisk, jovial and American, enters R., smoking a cigar and mopping his forehead. He is followed by* MARY CLARK, *his secretary, a serious and efficient woman of about forty, who looks tired and ill. She may be either American or English. After her comes* TONY, *a young American, carrying a film camera and tripod. Until near the end of the play, he is one of those slouchy young men who regard everything with indifference except their job, which they do with an efficiency not to be guessed at by their manner. He chain-smokes cigarettes.*

HAMBERGER. 'Mornin', folks ! (*Laughing.*) I guess there's nothin' like curiosity for rousin' you up outa bed.

SUSAN. Curiosity——

HAMBERGER. I'm Clint P. Hamberger, of Western Hemisphere Pictures, Incorporated. Guess you've seen my name of'n enough.

MARTHA (*awed*). Oh ! Do you make pictures ?

HAMBERGER. Well, lady, we don't deal in babies' bottles. Where's this guy—what's his name ?—Garth ? He won't let us down, I hope.

SUSAN (*seriously*). *He* won't let you down.

[HAMBERGER *goes to the upstage edge, briskly, looking down. Then he glances round and up towards the top of the mountain.*

HAMBERGER. Get a few shots of this while we're waiting, Tony.

TONY. Light's bad, boss.

HAMBERGER. Aw ! Risk wasting a few feet. Get it dim now—mysterious. We'll retake later when it's light. We can build up the story from that. And a shot or two of these people waiting in the half-dark. (*To the others.*) Mind posing, folks ?

[TONY *has begun to erect his camera and study his surroundings.*

PHYLLIS (*fluttered*). What? Are we going to be filmed?

MARTHA (*excited*). Oh! This is a thrill!

ROBINS (*cautiously*). Er—best think a bit——

[*The others do not reply.*

HAMBERGER. I'll say we're in luck! Just the craziest accident put us on to this—a breakdown in that one-horse little place. Wish we'd a full unit here, though. Want a coupla extra cameras and some lights. (*To* MARY.) Mary, you might get going on a bit of background description for the narrator. Begin with the mystery of the dawn—you know the dope. (MARY *remains still and serious.*) Look alive, honey! What's biting you?

MARY. I don't know. I—I feel—well—scared——

HAMBERGER (*surprised*). Scared? (*Laughing.*) Well, what can you take for that? (*To the others.*) We've shot charging lions and active volcanoes. We've been among pretty near every vicious kind of savage God ever let loose—cannibals, head-hunters, witch-doctors. We've been—aw, the hell to everywhere! (*With a gesture of giving it up.*) And here she is, among a lot o' simple Cook's tourists on a mountain—scared! Can you beat that?

ROBINS. We ain't Cook's tourists——

MARY. But suppose—suppose this does happen?

HAMBERGER. Happen? Nuts! The man's a crank. But cranks make good stories.

[MARY *sits on a rock, taking out pencil and notebook. But she does not write. She sits looking straight before her.* TONY *has started making shots of the mountain at various angles. He does so at intervals, moving his camera about from place to place, stopping to consider his material with screwed-up eyes and drooping cigarette.*

Now, folks, if you'll be so good as help me make a group——

ROBINS. But—look 'ere, mister, that'll be a sort o' legpull, won't it? I mean, in your language, the joke'll be on us. I mean, waitin' up 'ere f'r summat as never 'appened.

PHYLLIS. Oh! You mean—people will recognize us and think we were just silly?

DELPHINE (*anxiously*). Is it that? Just silly? Isn't—isn't it going to happen at all?

[*She looks desperate, on the edge of tears.* SUSAN *smiles and holds out her arms.* DELPHINE *goes to her.* MARY *gives a sad little smile at them.*

SUSAN. Don't fear, child. (*She takes* DELPHINE *in her arms.*) Why, you're cold! You should have dressed more warmly.

JEANNE. The poor little one has no money.

HAMBERGER (*suddenly, to* SUSAN). Hold that pose! Mother love—that's the stuff! Never fails with the great big warmhearted public. That's colossal! (SUSAN *and* DELPHINE *take no notice of him. He begins to try to group the others.*) Now you, lady—if you'll just——

SUSAN (*looking up*). You are wasting your time.

TONY (*turning his camera*). This wants music, boss.

HAMBERGER. Sure! We'll have Jalowski on to it.

[TALBOT DRENNAN, *an artist, and* MARILLA, *his wife, a dancer, enter* R. *They are young, intelligent, vivid. She is beautiful. He is English. She may suggest French, Austrian or Russian as desired, though with only a light accent. They are dressed in an attractively exaggerated style.*

DRENNAN (*hearing the last lines*). Why not Beethoven?

HAMBERGER. Beethoven? I've heard of him, though you don't think so. What about him?

DRENNAN. He wrote music—for this. (*He looks about him, appreciatively.*) God, what a setting! (*Pointing off backstage.*) That's Jungfrau, over there. I'll make a ballet out of this. Yes, Beethoven's the man. Dawn—the first dawn——

SUSAN (*puzzled*). The *first* dawn?

DRENNAN (*inspired*). You are the first woman, Marilla, in the dawn of the world. Eve, fresh from Adam's ribs. He is asleep—you wake him. He is afraid of you. He tries to struggle away, up the mountain. You tempt him down. You get him and take him lower down. We'll have Aluna Saschia for your friend the serpent, and a *corps de ballet* of angels and devils——

MARILLA (*inspired*). The dawn of the world! And I, dawn-woman, meeting the son of a god——

[*She springs lightly on to the rocky platform backstage, spreading her arms to an imaginary lover.*

SUSAN (*concerned, to* DRENNAN). Why did you come up here?

DRENNAN (*lightly*). For this—for inspiration. Or for adventure—the unusual attracts. (*Wickedly.*) More likely because Marilla fell in love with that chap Garth's eyes.

MARILLA (*turning*). He is a very handsome young man.

DRENNAN (*lightly*). Grounds for divorce already—and we've been married only a fortnight.

[MARILLA *laughs and springs from the rock into his arms. They are very much in love.*

HAMBERGER. See here, folks—I want you in this picture. (*To* MARILLA.) I guess I know you. You were in the International Ballet. Didn't we offer you a contract?

MARILLA (*wickedly*). Yes. Don't you remember what I told you to do with it?

[DRENNAN, MARILLA, HAMBERGER, *and* ROBINS *laugh.* PHYLLIS *giggles.*

HAMBERGER (*easily*). Well, no bones broken. And I'll say I'm glad to have you here. One big name, anyway. —Er what is your name?

MARILLA (*mocking*). So big you must ask? (*Waving at* DRENNAN.) This is my husband, Talbot Drennan.

HAMBERGER (*nodding to* DRENNAN). Glad t' meet ya. But——

MARILLA. You do not recognize him? He is the artist —far more famous than I am.

HAMBERGER (*still easy*). I wouldn't know. Artists don't get far with our public.

MARILLA (*still mocking*). But dancers are—commoner clay?

DRENNAN (*laughing*). Don't tease him, Marilla. He hardly knows Beethoven.

HAMBERGER. Wasn't he dead before I'd have had a chance to meet him? (*Impatiently, as they laugh again.*) Aw, cut it out! Time's passin'. I want these preliminary shots before this guy comes. Where is he, anyway?

DRENNAN. Yes, where is he?

SUSAN (*urgently*). Oh, please, all of you! Stop this and be serious. You have so little time to prepare yourselve..

DRENNAN (*surprised*). Why—she means it——

MARY (*quietly*). She's right. I can't help feeling she's right. Ever since I listened to Mr. Garth——

HAMBERGER (*easily*). Now now, Mary! Don't you go getting crazy ideas at your age. (*To the others.*) Mary's never fallen down on a job before—and what jobs! This is only a flyblow.

PHYLLIS (*nervously*). Is she your secretary? You know, I always thought you film—er—gentlemen had blonde secretaries——

HAMBERGER. Sure! We keep a few blonde lovelies for show, for publicity—and so on——

DRENNAN (*mocking*). And so on——

[DRENNAN, MARILLA, ROBINS *and* HAMBERGER *laugh.*

HAMBERGER. But when there's work to be done, it don't matter what colour they run to, or what their legs are like. In fact, the harder they are on the eyes, the easier they are to work with. (*Laughing, to* MARY.) Don't mind that crack, Mary.

[*But* MARY *is deep in thought and takes no notice.* VALERIE KEMPTON *enters R. She is well-dressed, greedy, adventurous; in her late thirties, still good-looking in a hard way, her hair peroxided, her voice penetrating.*

VALERIE. Oh, I'm not too late—perfect ! Such a struggle to get out of one's warm bed at such a perfectly ghastly hour ! (*Seeing the camera.*) Oh, are you taking pictures —divine ! You'll put me in, won't you ? I'm the Honourable Valerie Kempton. (*She addresses herself to* HAMBERGER *as the most important person there in her opinion.*) You'll have seen my picture often. Last week's " Tatler " had quite a nice one. But where is this Mr. Garth ?

HAMBERGER. Not here yet, lady. Now let's get along with the job, for Pete's sake.

VALERIE. I say, you don't think it's a hoax, do you ? I mean, of course no-one would believe what he said——
SUSAN (*interrupting quietly*). I believe.

VALERIE (*ignoring the interruption*). But he obviously believed himself. It's quite an adventure, and there's so little new, nowadays. Flying's just a bore now they've made it so safe, and motor racing isn't what it was. Then nearly all the real exploring has been done. Have you read my " Amazon on the Amazon ? " You should—I'd film it for you. I should like a chance to fly to Mars in a rocket. But, failing that, this promises a little thrill——

SUSAN. You will have a bigger thrill than you want.

VALERIE (*insolently*). That's the second time you've interrupted me. Who are you ? I seem to remember meeting you in the lounge of that lousy little hotel.

SUSAN. Yes. You are not prepared for this.

VALERIE. Prepared ? I had a double brandy before I came out, and I've ordered the best breakfast those incompetent fools can do for when I get back.

SUSAN. Oh !

[*TONY has been taking a steep-angle picture of the mountain from right upstage R., facing L. He is standing higher than the others. He speaks casually.*

TONY. Somebody comin' down, boss. Looks like it's him.

[*All turn towards upstage L. with varying degrees of expectancy. Then* HAMBERGER *makes an impatient gesture.*

HAMBERGER. Lord's sake, let's get on ! (*Annoyed, to* SUSAN, *who will not pose.*) Say, lady, can't you co-operate ? This is important.

SUSAN (*facing him, quietly impressive*). Important ? In a few moments your camera and film—yes, and all these mountains—will be ashes.

[*All stiffen, looking at* SUSAN.

MARTHA. Oh !

PHYLLIS. Oh dear ! }

VALERIE (*lighting a cigarette*). Nonsense !

JEANNE (*quietly*). And we shall be—where ?

[*Pause.* ROBINS *shakes himself and laughs sheepishly.*

ROBINS (*to* SUSAN). Now, ma'am, you didn't ought to talk like that. Makin' a serious business of a joke, that is.

HAMBERGER. It's a whole lot of boloney. And do I know it's a whole lot of boloney ? Course I do. I'm no sucker. But it'll make a good sensational story, and I'm here t' collect that story.

DELPHINE (*awed*). S'sh ! He's coming——

[*They look L. again.* GARTH *enters upstage L. and comes on to the rocky platform backstage.* MARILLA, *near him, looks into his eyes. He is still and serious. Frightened by his expression, she backs away with a little gasp, into* DRENNAN's *arms.*

MARILLA (*softly*). Aaah !

[*Pause. All are momentarily impressed by* GARTH'S *stillness. Then* HAMBERGER *makes an effort to pull himself together. He moves a few steps towards* GARTH, *but his manner is less assured.*

HAMBERGER. Mr. Garth ? I'm sure glad t' meet ya. I'm Clint P. Hamberger, of Western Hemisphere Pictures, Incorporated, and——

[GARTH *raises his hand, a slight gesture.* HAMBERGER'S *voice fades out. He gapes at* GARTH, *shrinking back a little.*

GARTH. That is of no importance—now . . .

    The mountains wait, white and remote,

    Their massy thews and ribs of granite and iron

    Rooted, colossal, in solid-seeming earth

    And mailed in glittering ice. The light has carved them

    Into a thousand wonders of loveliness

    To our short vision not unworthy of

    The ramparts of eternal Heaven itself . . .

    What are they, now, more than our brittle bone

    And weaker flesh ? What more than the soft voices

    Of the cow-bells yonder down in the sloping meadows,

    Or the keen-tanged smoke of the autumn chestnut-husks

    Burning along the lake ? . . . What is important, now,

    Of all we knew of importance ? What is eternal

    Of all we reached toward ? The white heads of the mountains

    Are cones of paper ; the solid earth itself

    A candle-flame at daybreak . . .

[*With a change of tone, more directly.*

                    Why have you come here ?

THE WHITE HORSEMAN

[*Pause.   No-one answers.*   GARTH *continues, sadly* :

The time has gone for scoffing—or for prayer.

(*Impressively.*)

The light grows.   From span to span of the universe
Legions of Heaven gather, winged phalanxes
Wheeling and soaring, armed with the hail and the
  lightning,
Thunder and hurricane.   Their breasts are plated
With the bright diamonds of a myriad stars.
The deep silence is fragile about their ranks
As time wearies toward eternity.
The hands of the Four Horsemen are ready to
  loose the reins
Of the White Horse of the Archer,
The Red Horse of the Swordsman,
The Black Horse of the Measurer
And the Pale Horse of Death.
The Seven Trumpets are lifted.

OTHERS (*gasping*).   Ah !

GARTH.   Soon we shall hear them.

That blast shall split the earth, roll up the firmament
And drive the seas out from their ancient beds
Adown the deeps of chaos.

[*Brief pause.* GARTH'S *entrance has changed the others,
lifting them to a more heroic level.   Their concerns have
suddenly become majestic or terrible.   Their action is larger.*
TONY *has stopped taking photographs.   He has surreptitiously
removed his cigarette and trodden on it.   He and his camera
make a gaunt silhouette against the lightening sky.* HAMBERGER,
*also, has stopped smoking.   He loses some of his self-importance
and briskness, but gains in stature and dignity.* SUSAN,
MARY, DELPHINE *and* JEAN *make a quiet group of acceptance
somewhere downstage* L. *The others have been swept by*
GARTH'S *entrance into another group towards* R., *a still but
fearful group with more of angles and tension, a triangular
mass with* TONY *and his camera as its apex.* GARTH, *still
standing above them, adds quietly* :

This is the end of the world.

DELPHINE. The end of the world—of sorrow——

MARY.   The end of sorrow and pain——

SUSAN. The end of the darkness in which we have waited
    long,

    Too long——

JEANNE. Unready. None of us ready. But who should
    know.

    Will God judge act or intention?

MARY.   None of us ready.

    I see the truth, now. A moment ago I had thought
    I was resigned—prepared——
    Better than some and little worse than most.
    But now a light is shining into my heart,
    And what I thought a proper resignation
    Shows no more than a care of self, an eagerness
    To be done with flesh diseased, condemned—
        condemned . . .
    Six months the doctor gave me; six months and
        pain.
    I thought eternity better, and the calm stars.
    I thought of a soft night, long, deep and long,
    With no more pain . . .
    I thought *that*—no further out from self,
    But I know now——
    There is no road to the calm dark
    Save through the core of the fire.

    [*She drops to her knees.*

DELPHINE. I, too, have sought no more than escape from
    pain;

    From the unending grey, unending gall.
    Is it forever, then? Is pain no less than forever?

    [*She drops to her knees.*

SUSAN. Are self and sin so great that we must bear them

    Beyond the end of time and into eternity;
    Twin shame, staining, evermore revealed,
    An amaranthine flaw in a crystal bowl? . . .

I knew of this. I was the first to know it,
And was—self-satisfied . . . If I, by *that* light,
Could not see clearly into my own soul,

What hope for me—now ?

[*She drops to her knees.*

JEANNE.   What hope for any of us

Is known only to God, and He is good.
Perhaps He can laugh a little, even now——
And we must pray . . .

[*She drops to her knees.*

GARTH. Though He may laugh or weep, He ends this
        game He has played,
    Folding together universe on universe
    Like a coloured huddle of cards ; a game of patience
    That has—not worked out . . . Year on year I
        have known
    This day—the last. (*Wildly.*) Why was that know-
        ledge mine ?
    Why not some other man's ? I have run from it ;
        running,
    Found it meeting me always. I have fast barred
        the door
    Of my deeper comprehension, bolt on bolt secured,
    Then, turning, found it within the room behind me.
    I have failed of the burden of it ; the burden of
        Atlas
    Enlarged, inexorable . . .

[*He covers his face with his hands.*

DRENNAN (*interested*). What would you have us make
    Of your tangle of strange words ?

MARILLA (*fearfully*). The end of the world, you say ?

    Or but the dread beginning of the end ;
    The Thousand Years of Revelation—the plagues——
    The vials—the beasts ? Ah !

[DRENNAN *makes a gesture of confidence to* MARILLA,
then speaks to GARTH. *He is challenging, with interest
greater than fear.*

DRENNAN.   Listen ! We have come

Here to this dawn-lit height as a matter of interest.
Something there was in your words, in your per-
sonality,
Attracted us, artists seeking dramatic material,
Impressive *décor* ; something to set to music
That should be somewhat nearer worthy the highest
Than we have yet achieved ;
Something to lift the lives of the little people
To heights beyond monotony of existence ;
Give them glimpses of beauty ; purge them by
pity and terror ;
Tear their emotions away from the deadening layers
Of fat little comforts and thin little fears. We
have come
For this, and who shall belittle our quest ? The
world cries out
From its drab and grey and scarlet of pain and war
For the artist and what he conceives. Ours is the
right
To make the best we can of the highest we find,
Reverently, coming to beauty on our knees ;
For beauty is truth and truth is beauty, and both
Are all above us, yet in the range of the vision
Of someone, some day. Toward that day we
strive,
Without hope of more than a single step forward
And then—hand on the torch. That is our
justification . . .
But who can dare ask that we should throw to the
flames
All we have done, planned, shaped, and hope to do,
And hope for others to build on us ? We have
suffered.
Is all our pain for nothing ?
Would God, hammering His beauty out of chaos,
Have thrown His tools down, letting the dark flood
back
Before the sixth day of creation ? Will God
Ask this of us ?

GARTH (*looking at* DRENNAN).

> How do we know what God will demand of us ?
> Or what He may give ? Perhaps He changes our work
> For better ; our vision for longer ; with new mediums
> Giving perfection for imperfection . . . But this——

[*He includes the whole scene in a sweeping gesture.*

> I know, certainly—this will end to-day.

OTHERS OF THE R. GROUP (*protesting*). No !

MARILLA (*desperately*).

> It is too much to believe ; beyond the grasp,
> Of any mind. If death should come, soft-padding,
> Holding his glass with the sand run down, why then
> One might accept the inevitable—but we
> Are young and vivid, vital ! It is monstrous !
> We must reject it ! . . . Oh, but I fear—I fear !

[*She clings to* DRENNAN, *sobbing.*

ROBINS. How should we know of this ?

MARTHA.   How should we know,
> We who are ordinary folk ?

ROBINS.   Come to see what was doing
> For entertainment—free.

MARTHA.   And you frighten us.

ROBINS. The end of the world is a long way off in our minds.

MARTHA. We've read the Bible, of course, but—the end of the world !

> Why, that's for the angels and such, and the decent dead
> Who will rise from their graves—not for the likes of us,
> Living. It isn't decent. If it were true
> I'd say we'd been properly had, that's what I'd say,
> As I don't mind pointing out——

ROBINS.   Ay, and so says another.
     There's that to do, yet. Could you break up a
          business——
     Snap !—like a back broken ? Even the end of the
          world
     Should come in decent order, after due warning
          given.
     The shakiest firm, in ending, has the formality
     Of liquidation, even though its assets
     Are drowned in liabilities.

GARTH.   What ? Do you think
     God should provide a formal seven days' notice
     Of the world to be wound up ; its liquidation
     Involuntary, and any other business
     Such as the judgment of man and the colonization
     Of Heaven and Hell ? . . . So you have never
          read
     The Book of the Revelation ? There has been
          warning given
     More than your seven days.

MARILLA (*angry because of her fear*). You, with your flood
          of words,
     By what authority do you frighten us ?

GARTH. I have no power to compel your ears or your
          minds,
     Nor do I frighten you more than myself.
     But I speak truth. We are waiting.

[*Pause.   The others look uneasily towards sky and sunrise.*

PHYLLIS (*fearfully*).   Still——all still.

SUSAN (*wondering*).
     Eternity—rest—quietness—— ?
     We are like trees in a wood as night falls
     On a summertime—waiting—still . . .

PHYLLIS (*terrified*).
     No ! There is something dreadful in the stillness.

OTHERS OF THE R. GROUP (*whispering*). Dreadful !

VALERIE (*with a defiant manner to cover uneasiness*).

    I don't believe a word of what you are saying.

[*She moves a little towards* GARTH, *admiring him.*

    Prophets were surely never so good-looking
    In the old days of the Bible ?
    Dirty and hairy old men, and quarrelsome, weren't
      they ?
    Why don't you leave alone the dreary business ?
    No pay to prophecy, nowadays—or is there ? . . .
    (*Provocatively.*)

    I could make life more thrilling—with you. We
      could snatch
    The good of it ; the silks and jewels and fame ;
    The lovely perils of love and dangerous venturing ;
    The stored beauties of warm earth. Man and
      woman——
    Lawless—together—urging each other to greater and
      richer
    And lovelier foolhardiness ! We may be all but
      gods
    And cheat life by the speed and scope of our daring.
    We will dare and fight even our hardest peril,
    Satiety. What do you say ? I am beautiful.

[*She is now near* GARTH, *holding up her arms to him.*
He stares down at her sternly.

GARTH. You dare to speak of your beauty, here in this
      waiting ?
    The breath of time is held, and, in eternity,
    What part of you, what shred of body or mind
    Or shrivelled husk of a soul, can you drag to face
    The light of a white throne of judgment ?

VALERIE (*shrinking back from him, screaming*).   Liar !
    (*Passionately.*) How could you know—how could you ?
      How are you more than man ?
    Women have lived the best of their lives with you,
    Urgently, in your arms, when moments are years.
    Women have lived more gladly for your lips.
    Dare to deny that !

GARTH. I did not seek to be chosen
For this. I tell you I have no less to fear
Than the worst of you. Have done. We can only
 wait
In silence—and hope there is something in us better
Than the bad we know.

HAMBERGER (*ironically*). So God tears up his script
And burns His settings and properties ; calls it a
 flop,
The long story He made ? I have scrapped a film
Many's the time—but would I destroy a work
Laboured so painfully and so clean regardless
Of all expense, and still, shall we say, booked up
To capacity everywhere ? That would be plumb
 crazy.
Why, the thing's a success, colossal from any stan-
 dard——
Life ! Yes, sir, that's the word ! Life, and I
 love it !
I want my share of creation. I reckon man's due
To steal a little of God's fire, and I want
My seventy years at least. (*He laughs.*) The end
 of the world ?
Not yet—and certainly not for me.

GARTH (*quietly*). There are four
Down on their knees prepared.

 [HAMBERGER *stares at him, suddenly more impressed.*

HAMBERGER. And the rest of us ?
What of the rest of us ?

TONY (*who has been increasingly uneasy, suddenly*).
I had an old mother
Used to say her prayers morning and night,
And thrashed me when I forgot, when I was a boy.
I wish I hadn't forgot. A prayer would be handy
 now,
Only I can't think of a single word.

 [A SHEPHERD *enters R. and crosses towards L. He is
an old man, cheerful and placid.*

SHEPHERD (*as he crosses*). Good day to you all. Though the day's none so good, really. 'Tis tricky weather, uncertain as my old woman—(*chuckling*) and the Lord knows it can't be more uncertain than she.

[*He climbs up on to the platform backstage L.*

GARTH. Where are you going?

SHEPHERD. Why, sir, where should I go but up the mountain t' my sheep? Sixty year I been doin' that, all winds an' weathers, an' only twice lost a ewe in the snow. I've a pasture up there in a fold o' the hills— good grass and sheltered, but it won't always do. It won't do to-day, neither. I'll have t' take 'em lower down, over the other side.

GARTH. What do you fear?

SHEPHERD. Fear? I don't fear nothin'—just exercises my commonsense. The sheep must be looked to, silly creatures, when the weather's uneasy. I can't bring 'em down this way, on account o' this here ledge, but this is the shortest way up.

[*He gives an anxious look up the mountain, then continues :*

I wouldn't stick about up here, if I was you. 'Tis dangerous.

[*He is moving off L., when* GARTH *stops him.*

GARTH. Stay! You're giving yourself unnecessary work.

SHEPHERD. That I'm not! I trusts my instincts.

GARTH. Your instincts are right. But they don't tell you enough. At sunrise the world will end.

SHEPHERD (*stolidly*). That's for God to arrange. He must do what He thinks best about that. Meanwhile, I've got my sheep t' look after. Good day.

[*He plods off L., unmoved. The others stare after him.*

GARTH. If I were like that man——

DRENNAN. That's the worst of us all, we're over-civilized. We ought to have got back to the primitive things. I see it now—too late perhaps—that the highest good

Is in simplicity.   We over-elaborate
And overload our canvases, torture ourselves
By digging deep through what we are pleased to
    call
Subconscious lower depths of our minds, like children
Puddling in mud for play . . . The charcoal
    sketch——
A few lines slashed on the white face of a canvas——
Holds more of truth than the finished picture. I
Shall be different now—if——

[DRENNAN *also has become impressed by the general atmos-*
sphere.   He breaks off, fearful, then adds passionately :

                                    Why are we waiting here
Like beasts in a slaughter-house ?

MARILLA (*fearfully*).   Why ? For no deep reason
    Most of us came—and now—we are conscious of
        doom.
    Yet this is a dawn like any other dawn.

GARTH. This is a dawn toward which I have journeyed,
        knowing,
    For twenty years.

DRENNAN (*pulling himself together, again challenging*).

                        Toward which the world has journeyed
For countless million years ?   You'd have us believe
That all the glory and pain of the numberless
    years
Are to end here, like the snuff of a candle, and we,
A handful, mainly nonentities, on a rock
Above a little, tenth-rate Alpine town,
Alone aware of it ?   Oh, we are fools, we are fools !
If we take you at your word.   (*Fearful again.*)
                        Or are we fools
Not to accept—prepare ?

GARTH.   You must decide.
    I did not ask you to come—any of you.

[*The R. group are now in state of considerable uneasiness*
which expresses itself in a massed, mechanical protest.

THE WHITE HORSEMAN

THE R. GROUP (*together, staccato*).
>   Stop ! We have heard enough
>   Of your silly tale.
>   The world end, indeed,
>   Because you say it will !
>   The world's work goes on
>   Colossal ; the harmony
>   Of the universe is yet
>   Destined to be
>   Longer than you will see.

[*They continue, individually, in the same mechanical way.*

DRENNAN.   Man rose from primal ooze
>   And straightened out his back——

MARILLA.   Making himself a will
>   To hew a bitter track——

ROBINS.   Toward good, from lost beginning,
>   Slow but sure his way—

MARTHA.   More sinned against than sinning
>   Is what I always say——

TONY.   It ain't no easy job
>   To make a thing of life——

PHYLLIS.   Weariness, disappointment,
>   Frustration, pain and strife——

VALERIE.   We have our moments, true,
>   But we earn them every one——

HAMBERGER.   Getting no more than our due
>   Between the dark and the sun.

THE R. GROUP (*together as above*).
>   Suppose we haven't amounted
>   To anything very much,
>   There's yet a bit to say
>   For humanity as such.
>   We make our protest here :
>   Man's not yet had his day,
>   Not one of us is ready
>   For the world to pass away ;
>   We've still our work—and play.

GARTH. You are not ready. We are none of us ready and
never shall be. Suppose God gave the world a million
years more ? Would humanity improve ?

THE R. GROUP (*together*). Let humanity have a chance,
and see.

GARTH. It would not improve. More than three thousand years ago, Akhnaton, King of Egypt, preached
world peace. Two thousand years ago, Christ, the Son
of God, died to show man the way of love. They were
but two of the great teachers, there have been many
others. But has man learned the way of peace or the
way of love ?

[*The R. group bow their heads in silence.*

THE L. GROUP (*together*).

Now we are past decision and come to acceptance.
We have not done well ; we see, now, we have not
Given to life what might have been expected.
There is a higher and rougher path than the path
we have chosen.
Though our feet have been shackled, we know we
could have achieved
Some little more than we have . . .

SUSAN. The world has taken and moulded us into self-
occupied patterns.
We have considered ourselves and our little and
personal concerns
As more than the peril and pain of others ; more
than the sum of humanity ;

MARY. We have turned inward our gaze to our hearts
and their individual agonies ;
The cry of the wide world has reached us no more
than faintly at intervals
Through our own crying, loud and louder, self-
deluding and self-demanding ;

DELPHINE. We have been shaken and torn by fear like
the roots of the lone trees
In wilder storms than are usual. Fear has tangled
the strings of our hearts and our sympathies,
Blurring our vision of life. We have looked not
up nor out.

JEANNE. We have come to consider only the price of a
> cabbage ; the bargain
> Struck in the morning market ; the polishing up
> of furniture ;
> The bearing of children and nourishing them,
> washing their faces for school ;
> The growing struggle of balancing household
> budgets ;

THE L. GROUP (*together*).
> Yes, though the feet of our higher selves have been
> shackled
> More than the feet of some, by disadvantages :

MARY. By growing and mortal pain, and fear of death ;

DELPHINE. By poverty, itself a sentence of death ;

JEANNE. Monotony, and the unrelenting clutch
> Of the common round——

SUSAN.   And a loss of the sense of
> proportion
> Due to excessive introspection——

THE L. GROUP (*together*).   We see ;
> We see, now, that we cannot excuse ourselves.
> We cannot say that, with such and such advantages,
> We should have done better.   Therefore we wait
> With no appeal ; with nothing more than our hope
> Of the goodness of God in the end.

GARTH (*gravely*). So must we all wait,
> Good and bad,
> Aware and unaware,
> The merging of time with eternity.
> [*In a ringing tone, indicating the sky to L.*
> Look how the light grows
> Toward the last day of time !

[*The R. group have lost their antagonism, except* VALERIE,
*who is irritably nervous.   They speak now in a wistful half-
acceptance.*

HAMBERGER. I'd like to have made another film—only
one more——

DRENNAN. And I, my ballet. I can see it all——

MARILLA. And I, to dance it—not only for the expression of myself——

ROBINS. I'd like more time. So much to clear up at the office——

MARTHA. I don't call it fair, and we on 'oliday an' all——

PHYLLIS. I've never really had anything to regret losing. I shall miss the Sunday services, of course. Those in Heaven will be different——

TONY. I guess I never done much thinkin'. If a guy coulda known how right the old girl was with her prayers——

VALERIE (*hysterically*). It's too frightful ! And we're all accepting it like—like kids accept Father Christmas. We're letting it beat us. We won't accept it ! Come on, let's live !

[*She moves impatiently away from the others, a little upstage.*

HAMBERGER (*seriously*). Say, folks, I still feel kinda puzzled about all this—but maybe there's something in what this man says. I'll grant he's got a way with him, and I'm not soft-boiled. Suppose we're all set for Heaven or the other place—in a minute or two ?

OTHERS OF THE R. GROUP (*starting*). Ah !

HAMBERGER. My old pop taught me never to take unnecessary chances—except by way of a fair gamble. (*He moves upstage as he speaks, taking a wallet from his pocket, from which he removes a thick wad of bank-notes.*) I guess I c'n do without this ballast, in the circumstances. It's the wrong currency for Heaven. I'm no camel to go through eyes of needles—so here goes——

[*He throws the notes in a shower over the precipice.* VALERIE *jumps to stop him.*

VALERIE. No ! Are you mad ? Ah-h-h-h !

[*Trying to grab the notes, she overbalances and falls over the edge. She screams, her scream dying away in the great depth. All the others rush to the edge, staring down, then draw back, horrified, silent.*

HAMBERGER (*dazed, after a pause*). Now who'd a-thought —(*His nerve breaks suddenly.*) Wouldya say I killed her? (*He rounds on the others.*) Wouldya put that on me, for me t' face the judgment with? (*Hysterically.*) I didn't kill her—I didn't! How was I t' know she'd do that? God! How was I t' know?

[*He slumps on to a rock, covering his face with his hands, sobbing.*

DRENNAN (*wildly*). We must go down and find her. We must get an ambulance. Perhaps she may be alive——

MARILLA (*gravely*). There is no perhaps about a fall like that.

GARTH. It makes no difference—now.

PHYLLIS. Oh! You mean—if the end of the world—— (*Hysterically.*) Oh, I can't bear it! It's dreadful, dreadful, dreadful!

[*She goes off into a terrible fit of hysteria.* ROBINS *grabs her by the shoulders, shaking her.*

ROBINS (*shouting, his own nerve gone*). Shut up, woman! For God's sake shut up! D'you want t' send us all stark raving?

MARILLA (*desperately*).
    Quiet! We must be quiet! . . .
    Time like a spinning top, running down, rocking already,
    Slowing, rocking to fall—ah!——

[*She puts her hands to her mouth to silence herself.*

MARY (*quietly*). How many minutes more?

DRENNAN (*wildly*). Minutes—minutes—seconds—obliteration——
    Or fire, flood, earthquake, searing agony—judgment
    In a court from which is no appeal——

[*He breaks off.*

PHYLLIS (*calmer, but awed and tearful*).   God help us !
> Ought we—do you think we ought—a little prayer ?

[*They drop to their knees, one by one, except* GARTH, *who turns away from them and leans against the rock* L., *hiding his face on his arms.* DRENNAN *and* MARILLA *cling together as they kneel.*

MARILLA.   Shall we be separated ?

DRENNAN.   May we dare to hope—dare to hope for
> anything ?

DELPHINE.   Hope has outworn herself in her empty
> labour
> Trying to put a gaudy face
> On our little and hollow lives,
> But never filling the hollow, never stilling
> The empty echoes.

JEANNE.   We do not need hope, now.
> We shall know soon—we shall know.
> No work for hope in another world——

PHYLLIS (*fearfully*).   The trumpet !
> We shall hear the dreadful trumpet calling the dead !
> Oh, let it come and be over !   Let it be done !

MARILLA.   Nothing will ever be over, where time is not.
> That, perhaps, is our hell—to be doomed to endure
> ourselves
> Forever—changeless——

MARY.   Must we have pain, unending
> Under the glare of a crystal and gold eternity,
> With never the dark and the anodyne of death ?

SUSAN (*joyfully*).   Let us lift up our hearts to the morning.
> God said " Let there be light "
> In a lesser dawn——

OTHERS (*startled by the idea*).   A lesser ?

SUSAN.   The morning stars ;
> The Sons of God, rejoicing among the stars,
> And all the multitudinous glories of space,
> Shall gladlier sing the song of the infinite, now.

[*The others have bowed their heads, kneeling, some crouching.* GARTH *alone is standing, still in an attitude of great weariness and turning away from the rest.* SUSAN *is kneeling upright, her face lifted to the sky, which is now gold with the sunrise. There is a pause and dead silence, broken only by a muttered prayer from* JEANNE.

JEANNE. Holy Mary, Mother of God—pray for us now——

[*Her voice dies away. Again there is silence. Then* SUSAN'S *expression changes from faith and joy to doubt, then horror. She stiffens, then starts to her feet.*

SUSAN (*horrified*). Look ! (*She points backstage L.*) Look ! The sun is up—clearing the mountains——

[*The others look up, sharply.* GARTH *swings round.* And nothing has happened—nothing at all !

[*The others start to their feet, a tense group staring off backstage L.* GARTH, *on the higher rock, is looking in the same direction. Pause. Then* SUSAN *speaks accusingly to* GARTH.

You told us—at sunrise. You were certain—years ago —of the very day——

[GARTH *turns slowly to face the others. He has aged. His face is haggard.*

GARTH (*dully*). I—don't understand——

SUSAN (*bitterly*). You lied to us.

GARTH. No. I spoke from knowledge—certain knowledge. And yet—the sun is up——

[*The others have reacted variously :* HAMBERGER, TONY, ROBINS, MARTHA *and* PHYLLIS *with the violent anger that accompanies relief,* JEANNE *placidly,* MARILLA *bewildered,* MARY *and* DELPHINE *sadly,* DRENNAN *tense and waiting.*

HAMBERGER.

TONY.

ROBINS. } Nothing ?

MARTHA.

PHYLLIS.

[*Their anger turns on* GARTH, *who stands dazed.*

HAMBERGER. So you been having a game with us?

DRENNAN (*wondering*). Mass suggestion? Hypnotism? Some new trick?

HAMBERGER. Say, what skunk d'ya think'd play a low-down trick like that? I threw twenty-five hundred dollars over that cliff.

ROBINS. What d'ye mean by it? Scarin' people—tryin' t' scare me?

MARTHA (*to* ROBINS). Now p'r'aps you'll listen t' me next time. I told you 'twas nothin' but some soap-box fellow doin' a stunt. Draggin' me into it—on 'oliday, too! (*To* GARTH.) You ought t' be proper ashamed o' y'rself, that you did!

PHYLLIS. Oh dear! One believes one thing, then has to believe another——

HAMBERGER (*savagely*). See here, folks! He's nearly killed us, these last few minutes. He did kill one of us.

ROBINS. He ought t' be made t' suffer for it.

HAMBERGER. Yes—suffer! But no court'll make him suffer. They'd only think we were crazy. We been hoaxed. Don't matter why we came up here originally, he got us when we were here. A crank, that's what he is—a danger t' the public.

DRENNAN. Shut up, man! I'm glad! (*He hugs* MARILLA.) And he's given us an idea. We got what we came for.

MARILLA (*gratefully*). Yes. We have God to thank for that.

HAMBERGER (*not to be placated*). I'm not the one t' be taken f'r a ride this way. This ain't no ordinary joke. This'll mark us for the rest of our lives. We shan't be able t' forget it. (*Beside himself with anger.*) Let him suffer for it. Let him do what that poor silly woman did. (*He moves up towards* GARTH, *menacing.*) Go on—over the edge with you.

ROBINS.
TONY. } (*also moving up*). Yes! Over the edge!
MARTHA.

OTHERS (*some of the women screaming*). No !

DELPHINE (*suddenly alive*). No ! (*She darts upstage and throws herself between* GARTH *and his opponents.*) Fools ! He is suffering more than you ! Can't you see ?

[GARTH *gently puts her aside. He begins to speak.*

HAMBERGER, ROBINS, TONY *and* MARTHA *fall back from him, joining the others in a tense group facing him.*

GARTH (*quietly*). For twenty years I have known it,
    certainly——
    Knowledge growing, goading ! There is no ques-
    tion——
    Even now there is no question. Day and place
    and hour
    Are right . . . Oh, I have made no jest with you !

[*With rising anger.*

    Who or what has dared to jest with me ?
    What god or power of Heaven or earth or Hell
    Dare make so gross a jest ? (*Passionately.*) There
    is no crime
    In all the filthy calendar of sin
    Thus foul ! Oh, there's no Heaven and no Hell ;
    No god nor spirit of good—nothing but mockery
    And hollow laughter ringing round the spaces
    From some colossal sham of stone or iron,
    Soulless, holding the arches of the skies
    With no more than mechanical efficiency
    And the unthinking order of the machine,
    Until (*more sinister*) some little foulness, self-begotten,
    Spreading and growing as a separate life,
    A cancerous growth on nature, brings awake
    Some robot-brain, aborted, apt to no more
    Than to quench the spark of the divine in man
    Lest he should rise to knowledge of himself
    And see himself a god.

DELPHINE (*fearfully*).   Your words are wild ;
    Too wild even for this. Oh, call them back !

GARTH. Then tell me what should make a jest of me.

[DELPHINE *is silent.*

You do not speak.

DELPHINE. I have no answer.

GARTH (*bitterly*). Man
Has two weak joints in his armour—his sincerity
And what he calls his faith. Nothing can hurt him
So he believes in nothing.

(*He laughs wildly.*) I have been fooled
And yet am certainly right. How may a man
Be right and wrong at once? (*Horribly.*) A lunatic
Might compass right and wrong together——

DELPHINE (*horrified*). No!

GARTH (*dully*). There is no hope, no future, and no end.

[*He drops to his knees, burying his face in his arms.*
DELPHINE *goes to him, putting her hands on his shoulders.*

DELPHINE. Last night I lost hope, too. Then I heard you speaking in the street. What you said made me forget I was cold and hungry. But for you, I should have killed myself. You made me glad. I'm still glad. I shall go on.

GARTH (*looking up*). How can you go on—you? With nothing? You have almost as little as I.

DELPHINE. I'm not afraid—now. (*She takes his hand.*)
Look at the sun—the morning.
There never was a lovelier day than this.

[GARTH *rises. They stand together, looking off to L. backstage. There is a sudden dull roaring, off L. All start, looking off upwards to L., alarmed.*

HAMBERGER. What's that?

[*The* SHEPHERD *runs on L. backstage, in great agitation.*

THE WHITE HORSEMAN

SHEPHERD.   The avalanche !   The avalanche !

[*He pauses for an instant C., to point upwards to L., in terror, then rushes off R.   The roaring increases to a great volume.   The others, except* GARTH *and* DELPHINE, *are terrified.*

HAMBERGER (*screaming*).   He's right !   Gosh !   He's right, after all !   The end of his own world—and ours !

GARTH (*in a ringing voice*).   The White Horseman !

[*All except* GARTH *and* DELPHINE *have made a concerted movement towards R., as if in terrified flight.*   GARTH *and* DELPHINE *are still, looking upwards to L.   Quick Curtain. The roar of the avalanche continues for a moment, crescendo, mingled with majestic music, the grinding of rocks and crashing of trees.*

THE END

T. B. MORRIS

The Ribs of Argo

A Play in One Act

LONDON
FREDERICK MULLER LTD.
29 Great James Street, W.C.1

FIRST PUBLISHED BY FREDERICK MULLER, LTD.
IN 1948
PRINTED IN GREAT BRITAIN BY WYMAN & SONS LTD.
LONDON, READING AND FAKENHAM

The Ribs of Argo tied for second place in the recent Poetic Drama Contest of the Poetry Society, in which there were 118 entries.

THE CHARACTERS

AGLAIA ⎫
SEMELE ⎭ *women of Corinth.*

JASON, *an old man.*

PHRYNE ⎫
ACANTHA ⎪
CALLIRRHOE ⎪
DORIS ⎬ *maidens of Corinth.*
IRIS ⎪
LALAGE ⎭

MYRON, *a young man.*

LAIS, *a young girl.*

RHEA, *an old blind woman.*

CLEANTHES, *a councillor, father of Lais.*

MEDEA, *an enchantress.*

(*Note.*—If desired, three young men may be included in place of the three maidens last named. The men's names may be IOLAUS, LADAS and PHOCION. Or, on a small stage, the maidens may be reduced to two or four only, with suitable redistribution of their lines.)

THE SCENE

Near the Temple of Poseidon on the Isthmus of Corinth. Evening of a summer day of the remote past.

A seashore, with a background of rocks which provide a higher level upstage, and some rocks in the foreground to serve as seats and also help grouping on different levels. If desired, there may be a few old pine-trunks to L., as the Temple of Poseidon, the sea-god, which is imagined as off L., was in a pine-grove. Jutting out from R. up-stage is the fore-part of the skeleton of Jason's ship *Argo*, beached there many years before in honour of Poseidon and to commemorate the enterprise for the Golden Fleece. The stem, figurehead and ribs of the ship are gaunt against a sunset sky, and these tall and heavy timbers dominate the scene. Entrances R. and L. downstage, also through the ribs of the ship upstage R. and over the rocks from upstage L.

It will be observed that a very striking setting is possible, with the great timbers of the ship reaching as high as (or even above) the line of vision of the audience, and a cyclorama showing the changing colours of the sky through evening gold and rose to crimson and purple with the rising storm, and then to green and deep blue as darkness falls. On the other hand, the piece may be set simply in curtains, with a few stylized rocks and just enough of the vessel's timbers to indicate what she is—perhaps a beam or two combined with a painting of more of the timbers on a back-cloth. With a simple setting the sky effects will be imagined as offstage R., and golden sunshine to begin, changing to rose, crimson and greenish light later, will be thrown from that direction to strengthen the descriptive matter of the play. All possible use should be made of shadows of the timbers. It is intended that all movements should be somewhat formalized, with a suggestion of ballet in the groupings of the women and maidens.

THE RIBS OF ARGO

Appropriate music of harps and/or pipes. AGLAIA *and* SEMELE, *Corinthian women of middle age, enter R. and L. before the lowered Curtain. They move C. and turn towards the audience. The music stops. They speak formally, half-chanting.*

AGLAIA.　The years pass, and the praise
　　　　　Of men is an empty thing;
　　　And the unrelenting days
　　　　　Leave never a hope to wing
　　　　　And no song new to sing.

SEMELE.　They tell of a prince of old,
　　　　　Jason, the worshipped of man,
　　　Who brought the Fleece of Gold
　　　　　And bought of honour a span
　　　　　In the days when earth began.

AGLAIA.　Jason, the master of *Argo*,
　　　　　Bringing far over the water
　　　A golden and midnight cargo:
　　　　　The Fleece—and a king's daughter,
　　　　　Glory and love and slaughter.

SEMELE.　Who are we that should blame?
　　　　　We know that a bitter rod
　　　Lies hid in the hand of Fame;
　　　　　And Joy is second-shod
　　　　　With pain from the heart of God.

[Brief pause, then AGLAIA *and* SEMELE *speak together.*

AGLAIA.⎫*Argo*, lovely once, on Corinth's shore
SEMELE.⎭Rots into death, nor may adventure more.

173

[*Music.* AGLAIA *and* SEMELE *go off to* R. *and* L. *as the Curtain rises, revealing* JASON, *an old man who has suffered much, wearing a dark cloak, standing with his hand on the stem of "Argo," looking towards the audience. The music stops.*

JASON (*turning towards "Argo," caressing the stem and speaking as if to a lover, his voice sad*). Argo—beautiful! Quick and young you were, fresh painted blue and gold, with fifty oars and a brazen wall of shields. And I—and hope—were quick and young. So long ago. I have forgotten how long.

[*He drops to his knees, still clasping the timbers, his head bowed on his arms.* AGLAIA *and* SEMELE *enter together* L. *and sit on a rock.* JASON *remains quite still, almost one with the timbers.*

AGLAIA. I wonder why they come here, to dedicate themselves to the ruin of an old boat?

SEMELE. Who knows? A strange old custom. To the glory of Poseidon, I suppose.

AGLAIA. Poseidon is great. But—a new statue rather than an old hulk, I should have thought.

SEMELE. I suppose there is some tale about how it came here?

AGLAIA. Oh yes, there is a tale—perhaps a great tale. But I don't know it.

SEMELE. It can't matter much, now. The new things are better than the old.

AGLAIA (*starting, pointing at* JASON). See—there is a man!

SEMELE. A poor old man. He has been about here for some days. He sleeps here.

AGLAIA. What, in that old rotting ship? A cold and draughty place of nights.

SEMELE. Perhaps he is too old to feel.

AGLAIA. The old chill easily.

SEMELE. Perhaps he is already under the fingers of death, and so feels no more the winds of earth.

AGLAIA. Perhaps. Death must be the only friend of such as he.

[*Gay music of plucked strings, and laughter, are heard off L. AGLAIA and SEMELE rise and look off L., curious.*

SEMELE. They come to deck the ship with flowers, for the feast of Poseidon.

AGLAIA (*gripping her arm*). Look, the young lovers are with them.

SEMELE. Myron and Lais.

AGLAIA. So Lais has defied her father after all.

SEMELE. S'sh !

[*They draw back together to downstage L. as the music and laughter become louder. PHRYNE, ACANTHA, CALLIRRHOE, DORIS, IRIS and LALAGE run and dance on L. They are young girls, brightly dressed, crowned and garlanded with flowers. They are leading MYRON and LAIS, a young pair of lovers, by ropes of flowers. PHRYNE carries a wine-cup, ACANTHA a vase of wine, and CALLIRRHOE a lyre. The others have handfuls of flowers with which they are pelting the lovers. All are happy and laughing. The music stops as they enter. They run to the remains of " Argo," grouping there around MYRON and LAIS. For the moment they conceal the kneeling JASON. AGLAIA and SEMELE watch them with kindly curiosity.*

PHRYNE (*jumping on to a rock so that she is above the others*). Hail, ancient vessel, holy charge of great Poseidon ! We pour a libation to thee.

[*She holds the cup towards ACANTHA, who fills it, then raises the cup in both hands and pours a slow stream of wine on to the sand.*

Hail, Poseidon ! Hail, great ruler of the seas ! (*Her voice becoming full of mischief.*) We bring thee two lovers (*pointing at the lovers in turn*)—Myron, who is well enough as men go, and Lais, who is much too good for him, as women always are.

ACANTHA. Grant that their quest of life be golden and fulfilled.

CALLIRRHOE. Thou who makest the storm and quellest it, give them safe passage (*laughing*) over the stormy waters of marriage.

[*All except* JASON *are laughing now.*

DORIS. Seeking only each other's arms upon the way——

IRIS. With never even an idle glance elsewhere, and never a cross word——

LALAGE. And never even a thought of regret——

PHRYNE (*mock-solemn*). What a hope !

ACANTHA. Well, we've done the best we can for them, and may their children be beautiful——

CALLIRRHOE. And many.

PHRYNE. Not too many.

[*Still laughing, they drag* MYRON *and* LAIS *downstage C., leaving them there, and begin to deck the remains of* " *Argo* " *with their flowers and garlands.* JASON *is again visible. He rises, wearily, looking up at* " *Argo.*"

JASON (*ignoring the others*). I can see thee yet
As that young time beheld thee. But never again
See Jason as he was——

MAIDENS (*reacting in a concerted movement*). Jason ? Who are you, stranger ?

JASON. An old man.

PHRYNE. And what of Jason ?

JASON. Nothing.

MYRON. Who are you, sir ?

JASON. An old man, as I have said, and best forgotten. Why do you deck the ship with your flowers ?

PHRYNE. We do not know.

JASON. The best reason for doing anything—that you do not know. There are no regrets that way.

ACANTHA. You talk strangely.

CALLIRRHOE. We have brought a pair of lovers for the blessing of Poseidon. Will you add your blessing to the god's ?

JASON. Lovers?

PHRYNE. You were a lover once, no doubt?

DORIS (*giggling*). Though it must have been a long, long while ago.

JASON (*quietly*). I was a lover—once.

[*He moves downstage to face* MYRON *and* LAIS, *who look at him with some uneasiness. The* MAIDENS *group behind him. They have been giggling at* DORIS' *remark, but suddenly become silent, tense, fearful.* JASON, *continues, bitterness in his voice :*

I could tell a tale such as never was told again in all the world.

MAIDENS. Tell us!

JASON. I shall not tell you.

PHRYNE. Then, as you are evidently someone of importance——

LALAGE (*interrupting*). Or think you are——

PHRYNE. Bless our pair of lovers. Your blessing should be of value.

JASON. Bless lovers? Curse them, rather. May they shun each other and remain virgin, that there be no such dreadful marriage-fruit as I have known.

OTHERS (*reacting, a gasp of horror*). Ah!

JASON. The faithlessness of man. The dark sorceries of woman.

MYRON (*pulling himself together*). You are too hard on lovers, old man. Your veins have been cold too long. All men are not faithless. I am not.

LALAGE (*laughing*). Not yet.

MYRON (*taking no notice of the interruption*). And, if women are witches, do we not like them so? The enchantments of love——

JASON. What of the enchantments of hate?

LAIS (*frightened*). I don't like him, Myron. I'm afraid of him. Come away!

JASON (*appraising* MYRON). You are strong. Perhaps you are brave.

DORIS (*giggling*). Any man who marries is brave.

JASON. You will grow to such a man as might have sailed with me.

MYRON. Sailed—where?

JASON. No matter.

MYRON (*coldly*). It is easy to guess. From your words now, one judges that your voyage was to hell.

PHRYNE (*fearfully*). Yes, yes! That is where he went. He comes from there—he has not wholly come from there——

ACANTHA. He has seen evil things. Their evil remains with him. The smell of death is on him.

CALLIRRHOE. He is dangerous, polluting life.

PHRYNE. Let us take him to the authorities and have an explanation.

DORIS.
IRIS. } Yes, yes! To judgment with him!
LALAGE.

[*The* MAIDENS *approach* JASON *to grip him. He drives them back with a wide sweep of his arms, and retreats upstage to stand with his back to the timbers of "* Argo."

JASON. Back! Am I, who have endured all else, now to endure your paltry Council of Corinth?

MYRON. You ask for trouble, with your evil words.

JASON. My words are good, and for your good, young man, if you but realized.

MYRON. Your words are dark and evil and old and afraid. I see now that you are one of those who have never lived, save in the imagination, because you have been afraid to live. You are one of those who sit ever in the shade because they fear the sun. (JASON *bursts into great gusts of bitter laughter.*) I am not afraid of you.

LAIS. But I am! Come away, Myron——

MYRON (*putting an arm about* LAIS). This is my wedding-day. (*To* LAIS.) You've defied your father for me. Shall a wretched old man frighten you?

[RHEA, *a very old, blind woman, hobbles on upstage R. between the ribs of " Argo," feeling her way with a stick.* JASON, *interested by what* MYRON *has said, stops laughing.*

JASON. So she has defied her father for you?

MYRON. She has. And in her I have all the world.

JASON. I knew another who defied her father—one who defied her father, and the world, for me. She brought more beauty than you will ever know, and a rich and strange dowry. You cannot know such treasure, but you will know the pain. There is no pain so great as that which comes to lovers ; no disillusion so complete as the knowledge that comes to lovers ; no hell so deep as that awaiting fools who love.

[*He turns abruptly and goes off upstage R. through the ribs of " Argo," passing near* RHEA, *who has been looking eagerly in his direction, head up as if sniffing the air.*

PHRYNE (*dryly*). You have been warned, Myron.

LALAGE. The wicked old rascal !

CALLIRRHOE. He should be locked up.

DORIS. Evidently he has been crossed in love.

ACANTHA (*serious*). Leave him be, to go his ways.

RHEA. Who has just gone from here ? Who ?

PHRYNE. I think we are well rid of him.

RHEA (*urgently*). Who passed me close ? There was greatness here—or the ghost of past greatness. Who was it ?

CALLIRRHOE. Only an old man.

RHEA. Nox, daughter of Chaos, has taken my eyes. But the old do not see with the eyes alone. There was a golden light about his head.

PHRYNE. We saw no golden light.

LALAGE. Is he, then, a god? Have we been entertaining a god?

DORIS. The gods choose many shapes (*laughing*), but who has ever heard of one choosing the shape of an *old* man, when maidens were about?

IRIS (*laughing*). Or visiting half a dozen maids at once?

LALAGE (*laughing*). Gods—like men—prefer us one at a time—alone.

RHEA. Enough! You and your silly little tales and thoughts of love! Do you think the gods have no better things wherewith to occupy themselves? Are you Leda, or Europa? Because your bodies are pretty and smooth you think you may mock at life. But I am old. I can remember three or four generations of such as you are—on your little journey from the kisses of men to the kisses of worms.

PHRYNE. And who are you, who have grown so far from the kisses of—men?

RHEA. My name is Rhea, but what is it to you? I have made a long journey hither, seeing without eyes, to stand once more by *Argo*.

OTHERS (*puzzled*). *Argo*?

RHEA. So you have forgotten! So little is the memory of the world for deeds of greatness. Ohe! I am old, and of no more use to any save death, but I keep a proper reverence for the great.

PHRYNE. She is mad—mad as that old man——

RHEA. That old man, whose name you did not ask; whose name you did not care to ask.

ACANTHA. We asked. He would not answer. He was ashamed of his name.

LALAGE. And we have nothing to do with old men—— (*Giggles*.)

DORIS (*giggling*). Except *rich* old men.

[RHEA *turns to "Argo," groping with her hands for the timbers. She touches the flowers.*

RHEA. *Argo!* They deck you still with flowers, then?

[*The others are tense, interested, turning towards* RHEA.

AGLAIA. Listen! She is giving a name to the old ship.

SEMELE. *Argo!* I've heard that name before—somewhere.

RHEA (*turning downstage to them*). Is there one who has not heard the name and the fame of *Argo*—of the Golden Fleece? Is there one who has not heard the name and the fame and the shame of Jason?

OTHERS. Jason?

PHYRNE. The old man spoke of Jason.

RHEA. It is the purpose of life that man shall quest the high and the beautiful; that man shall reach and seek beyond his power to find and grasp; that, like the unicorn, man shall die for beauty.

PHYRNE. She talks in riddles.

ACANTHA. The very old are often like that. The gods make them mad in the ending of their days.

RHEA. Lord Jason went with the Heroes in *Argo*, that fleet and lovely ship, sailing afar to a land barbarian and evil, to bring the Golden Fleece.

SEMELE. So that is the old tale.

AGLAIA. I knew there was a tale.

RHEA. Your mothers' mothers knew it. But the command went out that it should be forgotten on men's tongues and in their hearts. The worm is in *Argo* and the weeds have grown about her.

PHYRNE. Why should it be forgotten? It is a good tale and a great. Lord Jason brought back the Golden Fleece.

RHEA (*ominously*). And more. (*Pause.*) He brought the Fleece, not by his own strength and courage, but by a woman's enchantments.

MYRON. What matter, so he brought it? I think the tale a good one—a tale of heroes. (*To* LAIS.) We are together on a golden day—on our own golden quest, for joy.

LAIS. Perhaps joy is not for seeking. I am afraid.

[*She throws herself into* MYRON'S *arms, burying her face in his shoulder.*

RHEA. Lord Jason should have looked to his own courage, and not to a woman's arts. Then his adventure might have had a different end.

ACANTHA. Yet he succeeded. He brought back the Golden Fleece.

RHEA. But what more did he bring? Ask that of Jason, where he wanders alone over the bitter earth. Ask of Medea, witch-daughter of a barbarian king.

OTHERS (*in a concerted reaction, fearfully*). Medea? What have we heard of Medea?

RHEA (*ominously*). Let man beware the fulfilling of his quest.

[*Brief pause. The* MAIDENS *are in a tense group, standing, crouching, kneeling, staring at* RHEA. MYRON *is still holding the frightened* LAIS *in his arms.* AGLAIA *and* SEMELE *are a little downstage and to L. of the others, standing together.* RHEA *is standing on a rock above them, against the timbers of " Argo." The light has dimmed and become rosier, in a sunset promising storm.* RHEA *laughs quietly, evilly.* LAIS *breaks from* MYRON'S *arms and runs towards L.*

LAIS. I cannot stay here! It is a fearful place!

MYRON (*darting after her*). Lais! For nothing but an old woman—an old man——

[LAIS *is just about to run off when she is faced by* CLEANTHES, *her father, a fat and prosperous councillor of middle age and languid and affected manners.*

LAIS (*recoiling*). Father!

CLEANTHES (*in a gentle, almost pleasant voice*). So this is where you are? And already you are afraid. What did I tell you? Do you see, already, the wisdom of my advice—of my commands?

MYRON (*again putting his arms round* LAIS). She is no longer yours. She is mine.

CLEANTHES (*still pleasant*). So? Always impulsive, young man. Still too headstrong to notice that she will be of little use to you dead (*laughing gently*), especially as you will be dead also. (*The others are all looking towards them.*) Little fool! I thought I had frightened you out of this mad prank.

LAIS (*hysterical*). I won't go back with you—I won't! I'd rather die!

CLEANTHES (*gently*). Ridiculous! You have pleasant food and a soft couch with me, and clothes to fit your looks. Will you rather have rags and a crust and the hard earth with this—(*laughing*)—this nonsensical young man? (*Significantly.*) Always provided you get that far.

LAIS. I will have anything rather than your house. I will have death rather.

CLEANTHES. Tut tut! And my good friend Glaucon— my very good, rich friend Glaucon—waiting to make you his wife.

LAIS (*shrinking back against* MYRON). Ah! Kill me, Myron! Kill me before he takes me.

CLEANTHES. Oh, you may spare him the trouble of that. I have no doubt he would find the task extremely distasteful—at this stage in your relations. (*His voice is still smooth, languid, almost friendly except that there is a sinister ring to it.*) Either you return to Corinth with me and accept my worthy friend Glaucon—ah, what money-bags!—as your husband, or I shall exercise my right of killing you myself. (*With a note of sadistic appreciation.*) To kill one's own daughter—a new and perhaps almost agreeable experience.

LAIS (*and all the others, except* RHEA *and* MYRON, *horrified*). Ah!

MYRON (*whipping out a dagger*). Devils of hell! You are mad! She is mine. She goes with me, far from this place and that vile old man you'd sell her to. (*He *moves forward, menacing* CLEANTHES, *pushing* LAIS *behind him.*) We'll see who is going to die.

LAIS (*fearfully, clutching* MYRON'S *arm*). Myron! No! He is my father. Will you bring down the anger of the gods on us?

RHEA. Patricide! The Furies wait upon such deeds.

CLEANTHES (*easily, not shrinking from* MYRON). How far do you think you will get with her? Be sensible, young man. Look at the matter as I do. One should always consider the point of view of the other person—that is a principal virtue of the enlightened. Think of me, then. Am I to sit with the great in council—myself, mark you, as great as any—and sense men whispering just beyond my ears; whispering that Cleanthes' daughter has run away with a mere fellow?

MYRON. She is going with me.

[CLEANTHES *flicks the dust daintily from a rock near him, and sits, smoothing his robe.*

CLEANTHES (*still easy*). To her death, then—and yours. All your paths will be blocked, and every boat withheld. (*Very satisfied with himself.*) Oh, I have not my power for nothing. With Lais, you are a doomed man already. Think well, young man. Is your life worth no more than one woman's body—even my daughter's?

MYRON (*to* LAIS). Let me kill him.

LAIS. No, no!

CLEANTHES. There are plenty of women—beautiful for a little when they are young. Be reasonable, now, and you may choose for yourself among my virgin slaves. I have a very nice—er—collection. You are not yet ready for the responsibilities of marriage (*with an evil chuckle*), but not too young for the privileges of love— oh no! (*As* MYRON *makes a gesture of distaste.*) Hasty again? Think further. Think how this girl has deceived and disobeyed me, her loving father. Will she not deceive and disobey you also, one of these days, when she is tired of being the wife of a poor man, and hunted over the earth as well (*chuckling*)—*if* you get past my guards?

[*The evening has grown darker. An uneasy wind begins to whisper fitfully.*

SEMELE (*fearful*). There is something in what he says.

AGLAIA (*fearful*). Death is a hard price to pay for love.

PHYRNE. Yet love is the great adventure of youth. It should be sought in the morning of life.

ACANTHA. Those feeble ones who wait until noon are apt to find that the day has turned out rainy.

CALLIRRHOE. Rain? We are going to have a storm, soon. Look at the sky.

RHEA. There is no morning here, save in their youth. And youth falls to the knife as quickly as age can do. And quicker to the knife of disillusion. (*Cackling.*) Ohe! (*Sinister.*) Listen! The wind is but hardly held in leash. The gods are beginning to whisper in their far places.

DORIS (*fearful*). It will be dark soon, and cold.

IRIS (*fearful*). I do not like this place when night falls.

LALAGE. I am afraid.

LAIS. Take me with you now, Myron.

CLEANTHES. He can take you but a little way. He is a dog tethered by a short rope. (*Laughing.*) Soon he will be a dog hanged on a shorter one.

[RHEA *joins* CLEANTHES' *laughter. All turn to stare at her.* JASON *enters between the ribs of* "Argo" *and stands quietly near her. The light dims considerably, and from now on the stage is darker generally, though shafts of late sunlight strike across backstage from R. to L., silhouetting* "Argo," RHEA *and* JASON, *leaving the others in varying degrees of shadow.*

RHEA. Ohe! I have eyes in my ears, in my fingers, in my nose. I see death more strongly by the smell of death. Look at the sky, violent and strange. The savage guardians of the gods mass in the western sky.

[*She gestures R. The others react, fearful.*

IRIS. How does she know that?

RHEA. I feel a gathering of power. Something is here that was not here before. I am an old woman who has seen many things. Without eyes have I seen them. But only once have I seen another night like this—the night Medea left Corinth.

JASON (*a great and bitter cry*). Medea!

OTHERS (*in fearful whispers*). Medea!

RHEA. The sky was a strange flame. There were great dragons in the sky, as those which now contend above us in the clouds. (*Pointing upwards.*) I saw what she did——

JASON (*crying out in agony*). Ah, gods!

RHEA. I saw all she did——

[*The wind rises suddenly. The timbers of " Argo " strain and creak.*

Medea the sorceress! (*The words jerked out fearfully to a scream, crescendo.*) There are crimes unnatural, and one above all others to be abhorred! (*Whispering.*) Listen! The timbers of *Argo* complain at the name of Medea.

OTHERS (*fearful*). Ah!

[*The wind hisses up to a quick fury, then is suddenly still. The shafts of sunlight disappear, so that the stage is nearly dark.* MEDEA *rises on to a rock upstage L., a tall, commanding figure in a blood-red or purple cloak, dimly seen.*

MEDEA (*a quiet and beautiful voice, full of sadness*). Who calls Medea?

[*The shafts of sunlight appear again, striking full on* MEDEA. *She is standing higher than any of the others, a woman of great and mature beauty ; one who, but for her magic arts, would now be old, and who is therefore ageless rather than young ; a woman foredoomed to evil but taking no joy in it. The others have turned towards her and even* CLEANTHES *is tense.* MEDEA *continues :*

Let my name be known
Only along the wild complaining wind

From earth inclined towards chaos ; in the dirge
Of the sea's surge ; in the thunder
Whereunder the wrath of God is plain. Never
    again
Let my name live, but drown in the thunder and
    sea ;
Die on the wind, like the wind, fitfully—
Never again to be known to man and the men
    to be.

JASON (*bitterly*). Medea !   ⎫
OTHERS (*whispering*). Medea ! ⎰

RHEA (*whispering*). Sorceress !

MEDEA. Let me be known
    Only as one nameless, overthrown
    And driven from all joy, to live alone.

JASON (*bitterly*). Medea !   ⎫
OTHERS (*whispering*). Medea ! ⎰

RHEA (*whispering*). Sorceress !

OTHERS (*catching up the whisper, repeating and repeating it
quickly, irregularly, for a moment, so that it becomes one with
the wind which has begun to whisper again*). Sorceress !
Sorceress ! Sorceress !

    [MEDEA *raises a hand. The wind and whispering stop
together.*

MEDEA. You, when you make your prayer ;
    Your little shoots of wilting prayer from the sod
    Of your sterile souls, have no true name for God.
    You have never known His name.
    " O Zeus, Cloud-gatherer, Mighty Thunderer,
    By whatsoever name
    Thy pleasure would be that we should address
      Thee, God,
    Hear us ! " you cry. But *His* name is His Own
    Unknown—too high—echoing only—
    More lonely than ever loneliness of mine—

About the awful gulfs of the farthest sky. (*Pause,
  then, gently :*)
As He, for glory, so for my sin am I.

[JASON *takes a few steps towards* MEDEA, *amazed. The
others watch.* RHEA *is crouching on her rock, the other*
WOMEN *in a frightened group, towards R.,* MYRON *and* LAIS
clasped together downstage L., CLEANTHES *leaning forward
tensely on his rock, C.L.*

JASON. So you have dared to come
  Again to Corinth ?

MEDEA (*wearily*). As you have come.

JASON.   I have prayed
  Two prayers. The one for my own death. The
    other
  That never again, living or dead, in earth or hell,
  Should I come near you, woman.

MEDEA.   Woman, you say ?
  Woman—yes. And, because I am a woman,
  I have done—all I did. We are near the end
  And, ending, because I am woman ; only because
  I gave you so much more than any woman
  Has ever given to man, you shall hear me now
  A little while, in patience, waiting the dark.

JASON. I have no ears for you. I have only hands
  To kill you——

MEDEA (*quietly*).   A little patience, before the night,
  Then—you may—what you can. (*Passionately.*)
                          Should I not welcome death ?
  (*Fearfully.*)
  If, indeed, I may die. Is there a place on earth
  From which I am not an exile ? Or any place in
    hell
  Ready to give me home ?

JASON.   The gods have given to me
  What I asked not—and yet a larger gift
  Than my prayer asked. 'Tis greater than my hope,
  To have you here between my hands—now—
  That shall crush your life.

MEDEA. You have learned nothing, Jason. (*The others, except* RHEA, *start and draw back at the name.*)
You have not grown
In all the years, one small step onward. You have not gained
A little inch of experience. Your heart is the boy's heart
That drove the voyaging *Argo*. Your thoughts are the boy's thoughts
That comprehend yourself, your honour and glory,
Your quest, your argosy—nothing beyond yourself—
Least of all Medea, Princess of Colchis—fool
Who gave her body and soul ; who gave her hopes, all,
In this and every world, for you.

[JASON *moves nearer to* MEDEA. *She faces him unmoving.*

MYRON (*wondering*). What is here
Of witchery and woe ? What are these names to thrill
A man's nerves like the strings of a plucked harp ?
Jason—Medea ! Names forbidden——

RHEA. Forgotten.
Their names are part of chaos. The night is howling,
Rending their names forever as a wolf tears
The dead flesh from the bone.

LAIS (*urgently to* MYRON). Let us away, and far !
What though death be the end of the road ? Is there any
Having another end ?

MYRON. We will stay and listen.
Listen and learn.

LAIS. What need for you and I
To learn of love ? We have plumbed the depths of love
Who are willing to seek love in the deeps of death.

RHEA (*sardonically*). As lovers seek the dark,
  These greater lovers will seek the larger dark,
  A night too long even for lovers. What shall be
    said to them
  Who will not even open their minds to a truth ;
  A single, simple truth ? Warm blood in the veins
  Turns lover to lover—*only* that blood. But death
  Blows cold his breath over the blood and the heart
  And the once hot lips of lovers—cold—and cold
    the bed
  They know and never know, together, or ever
    apart,
  What matter ? The kiss of the hungry worms is
    all
  They shall ever and never know.

MEDEA.   The kiss of death
  Is faithful at least. Death does not change his
    mind
  As man does. Oh ! I have seen man make a
    glory
  Of what he had no purpose but to betray.

LAIS (*wondering, moving up a little towards* MEDEA). I do
    not know you, lady,
  But I do not believe all men
  Are as you have found one man.

MEDEA. Think what you will. You will grow out of
    belief,
  If death takes you not first. You had better pray
  To grow from love at the same time, and learn
  Indifference, so to avoid hatred.
  The greater the love, the darker the hate it breeds
  Certainly.

LAIS (*protesting*). No !

MEDEA.   Pretty and empty-headed,
  So you would measure with mine your small
    experience ?

[MEDEA *looks into* LAIS' *eyes.* LAIS *shrinks back.*

LAIS.   I am afraid of you!
   Who are you?   What have you done?

MEDEA.   I have loved—more greatly than you shall love,
   And so—hated.

LAIS.   Your still eyes hold the knowledge of all evil.
   The heads of serpents flicker above the pools,
   The night pools.   I will not look at your eyes!

[*She tries to cover her eyes with her hands, but vainly.
Fascinated by terror, she is compelled to gaze again into*
MEDEA's *eyes.*

   I—will—not—look——   (*Crying out.*)   Myron!

[MYRON, *who has moved up behind her, takes her in his
arms again.   She buries her face in his shoulder, sobbing.*
MYRON *faces* MEDEA, *who looks at the lovers for a moment,
sadly.*

JASON.   Enough of words!
   What have we here to do with love, on a night
   So charged with a greater purpose and dark with
      a greater dark
   Of the shadow of it?   To an end!

[MEDEA *looks at him again.   He takes a step towards her.
She gestures him back.*

MEDEA.   This moment is mine
   Towards which I have come from the boundary
      of the world—
   Farther, maybe.   You shall hear me.

JASON (*bitterly*).   I have heard you
   Too many hours in the years long gone, and the
      tale
   Was ever the same.

MEDEA (*wearily*).   Ever the same.   Of a woman
   Who loved, and a man who was false.

JASON.   Woman of midnight;
   You who have stored the evil of all the world
   To generate that which men must shudder from
   And the good light loathes—do you dare?

MEDEA.   I have always dared
For you—and once against you. (*Bitterly.*)
                            Oh ! I have offered
The blood of black ewe lambs and the sweet honey
To fearful Hecate in midnight groves.
I have dared seek the mandrake root ; enchanted
Spirits of moon-cold air and of dead earth
To teach me words of power, older than man,
Wherewith to blast power out of the womb of the
     world
As servant to my purposes. . . .
I have laid my spirit in pledge to the lower gods
And set my face to the dark, Jason.

JASON.   Enough !

MEDEA. Enough of words for you now. Enough of
     deeds
Never. I gave you all, but still you must goad
And stretch for more, till I failed. . . .
In the first day I knew you, I killed for you
The Never-sleeping—he would have killed you,
     else,
That ancient serpent-guardian of the Fleece—
So I fulfilled your errand.

JASON.   So dimmed my honour.
Had I not looked in your eyes, I had done the
     deed
Alone, and had the good of it. But you
Dimmed me the credit of the highest quest
Man has adventured on.

MEDEA (*with rising anger*).   Ah, monster ! You
Make light of love-gifts ; even of the dawn of
     love
When a princess came to you as a simple maiden
On Colchian sands. For you I left my home.
For you I left my father, forever. For you
I slew my brother.

[*A gasp of horror from the others.* MEDEA *goes on more
gently* :

Do you remember, Jason,
The long nights of the voyage back ; each hour
An hour nearer your home, farther from mine,
When you healed my hurt awhile ?

JASON (*brutally*).   I would to God
I had never seen you ! Now let us make an end.

[*Again he moves towards her. Again she gestures him back.*

MEDEA (*in a more sinister tone*). Do you remember, Jason,
        my reward
Here when we came to Corinth ? Do you re-
    member
Seeking a young and golden bride, while I
And the two sons I bore you——

JASON (*crying out*).   Ah !

MEDEA.   ——were to go
Into the cold of exile ? Do you remember
Speaking me false, the while you made your plans ?

[JASON *groans, covering his face momentarily with his hands.*
MEDEA *goes on :*
I had no father to avenge me. I
Had left my father's home. I had no brother
For I had slain my brother——

JASON (*passionately*).   You slew my faith.
You slew my bride and her father——

RHEA.   Death building on death,
Murder on murder teeming and battening, like
Those things that crawl and teem in the slime
    under
Old rotting stones——

MEDEA.   I killed your other woman.
Was it not just ? Hear me, you women of Corinth,
And say, was there no justice in her death ?

PHYRNE. Woman has need of justice against man
        Most times of her life.

ACANTHA (*fearfully*).   But there is more here
Than you have yet spoken——

RHEA (*cackling*).   Ay ! There is more.

193

OTHERS (*tense and fearful*). What is to come? O gods, what is to come?

JASON (*to* MEDEA). Do not appeal to justice. There is no law
Dare comprehend your crimes. As madmen brood
From broken shard to shard of their minds, conceiving
Things new and hideous, man would come to think
On mad, unnatural sins more than old tales
Have ever ventured on, did he think of you
And your last crime in Corinth.

MEDEA (*with satisfaction*). She died not easily.

JASON. I do not speak of her. She was young and fair,
A sweet means to an end—the throne of Corinth
After her father's death. I might have had that throne.
You could not share it with me—and I had lost
My right throne of Iolcus. Should I have clung
To a dark witch through the lingering years?

MEDEA (*sadly*). A witch
Who used her witchery only for you, for you,
Until you spent your treachery on me.

JASON (*impatiently*). You harp on that, as though man's reaching for woman
Was a matter of first importance. Are a man's eyes
To be bound to the beauty of one? And are his hands
And his strength for no more than one? The gods love many,
And man, in love, is a god, creating——

MEDEA. Ah!
You are indeed as you were. You excuse your sin;
Even glory in it. That is the difference
Between a man and a woman, Jason. Woman
Accepts what she has done—and suffers——

JASON. I——

Have I not suffered, then? . . . But I shall kill
you
Not for the crimes you have spoken of—but the
last—
After you killed my bride. (*Shuddering.*) It is not
to be named.
It brought a shudder of horror even to hell.

[*Pause. The others stiffen with a new fear.* JASON
moves a little towards MEDEA, *who remains quite still.*

There is no forgiveness ever for such a deed.

OTHERS (*whispering*). No forgiveness ever—no forgiveness——

[*The wind rises again in a sinister whisper, as though
echoing the voices.* MEDEA *raises her open hands, speaking
gently but with authority.*

MEDEA. O wind, be still again and sleep, for I
Have somewhat more to say—and my voice falters.

[*The wind dies down with startling suddenness. There is
dead silence for a moment, then an awed gasp from the* WOMEN.

WOMEN. Ah!

RHEA. She commands the elements.

MEDEA. I command
More than you know. (*To all the others* :)
I used my powers for him,
But he, taking my gifts, rejected me,
Making decree that I and my innocent sons
Should be banished straight from Corinth—lest we
meet
His guilty eyes too often, reminding him
Of that in which he had failed ; reminding him
Of children other than those his milky bride
Might scrape the strength to bear him, and re-
minding
His false heart of a woman whose veins ran blood ;
Who had given so much that never could he hope
To cancel the debt.

JASON (*grimly*).   The debt shall be cancelled.

MEDEA.   Peace.
> Your turn shall come again.   (*To the others :*)
>   The thing I did
> For which there is never pardon——

RHEA (*in horror*).   Do not name it !
> Do not speak of it—do not !

MEDEA (*to* RHEA).   What do you know ?

RHEA.   I was there.

> [*She moves nearer to* MEDEA, *her hands clawed out as if in
> supplication, bent, with halting steps.*

MEDEA (*staring at her*).   The old blind nurse.   Even then
>   you were old.

RHEA.   And blind.   But I saw.   Oh, never speak of the
>   deed !
> Let it go down to the hell from whence it came
> With no more than its own whispers.   Those are
>   enough
> To add to man's unease. . . .
>   (*More fearfully.*)
> If there are things frightful behind a door,
> Shall we unlock the door ?

MEDEA (*quietly, stonily*).   The door of my mind.

> [*Pause.* MEDEA *continues in a different tone, with a note
> of madness :*

> How still the night, now !   All winds and all the
>   seas
> Have held their breath to listen. . . . My sons
>   were lovely.
> In their eyes only, out of all the world,
> Was any love for me that day.   Pity I had
> From the women of Corinth, but never love from
>   other
> Than my two little sons.   They were all I had.
> And I—was all they had.

RHEA.   Princess !   Be still !
> The thing must not be told.

MEDEA (*ignoring the interruption*). I was all they had.
    They had not played me false, nor ever would.
    But what had life for them, exiled, disowned
    By him who should have cherished them ? And the
       man
    Who turned lightly from their arms and mine
    To the arms of a strange woman, should he be
      comforted
    By *her* children—(*a note of horror*)—by *any child ?*
    Should he not wander childless all his days ?

[*Pause. Dead silence.* MEDEA *adds quietly :*
    I slew the woman, and I slew my sons.

OTHERS (*a sigh of horror*). Ah !

MEDEA (*passionately*). *Now* let the heavens lament and all
      the winds
    Cry desolation ! It goes on and on
    This terror of longing, fixed in that eternity,
    That ultimate shape of hell, the circle. There is
      no end
    To what I pay. The doom of Ixion,
    Prometheus, Sisyphus, Tantalus, may ease
    In a thousand years or so, but I—Medea—
    Have respite nevermore. . . . (*Wearily.*)
    Where is your sword, Jason ? 'Tis not the first
      time
    Your steel has thrust against my heart.

[*The wind has begun fitfully to whisper and wail again.*

JASON.   A sword ?
    Long since I had a sword. Now all I have
    Are my two hands—a hangman's hands for you.

MEDEA (*quietly*). So ends man's gratitude.
    Well, make an end—if you may.

JASON.   An end to all.
    My *Argo*, gallant once, rots—for your sin.
    My life—no more than *Argo*, the bones alone
    Clinging in perilous determination
    Only so long as takes to make an end.
    No more to hold or desire. No more to hope.

MEDEA (*gently, mocking*). Yet such a boy you must expect
that Hope
  Shall cling to you when youth has gone? Ah,
   Jason,
  Hope gives her favours only to young lovers.
  Have you never learned how little of good a man
  May hope to draw from life? Have you never
   learned
  That the world was other than your plaything?
   Well,
  I have learned more. I am familiar
  With the pale narcissus of Hades, the dark cypress,
  And the reverberations flinging back
  From echoing concavities of hell
  The names of a man's crimes to his own soul.

JASON. Death, then, for crimes.

[*He moves quickly towards* MEDEA, *his hands ready to
take her by the throat. But* LAIS, *who has been watching*
MEDEA *with a new sympathy, springs with a cry between
them.*

LAIS.   No! She has known too much
  Of pain, already——

JASON (*recoiling*). What?

LAIS.   Let her go in peace——
  Or what, passing for peace, she may find on earth.
  In the name of love, let her go.

OTHER WOMEN (*except* RHEA).   In the name of love,
  Let there be no talk more of hatred and death.

[*The other* WOMEN *make a concerted movement L., as if
placing themselves at the side of* MEDEA.

MYRON (*protesting*). Lais!

LAIS.   Peace! You said we had much to learn,
  And I—am learning.

MEDEA (*gently putting* LAIS *aside*). I want no help from
  any.
  Death is not to be shunned by me, if he give me
  death.

I have gone far, far down the road of sorrow,
Alone, with no relief. The smiles of children,
The tender grace of leaves, the joy of pure giving,
The slow calm of the harp singing in darkness,
Or the strong hands of a lover, cherishing——
These are no more for me—no more. (*To* JASON :)
    I am ready.

[JASON *takes another step towards* MEDEA, *then stops.
His hands drop to his sides.*

JASON (*heavily*). I cannot kill you.

MEDEA. Give me death, and I forgive you all.

JASON. I cannot forgive you. I cannot kill you.

MEDEA. I feared it.

[MEDEA *looks steadily at* JASON, *who puts his hands before
his face to shut out the sight of her, and backs away to R.
until he is brought up against the timbers of " Argo." He
groans and, turning, clasps the timber of the stem, burying
his face on his arms.* MEDEA *goes on sadly :*

There is a bleak wall of power about me
That none may pierce. I have built up that wall
And it has trapped me. . . .

[*Facing* LAIS, *disillusion contrasted with young confidence :*

You who have come in love and have seen hate,
That worse hate which love breeds, now or to-
    morrow,
Which do you choose now ?

LAIS (*confidently*).   Love—now and forever.

MEDEA. There is no forever in love—only in hate.
More than all lovers, we had the world in our
    hands,
And we have shattered the world.

LAIS.   We have no great desires
Beyond each other. So will the gods be kind.

MEDEA. Until your lover sees another woman
As more desirable. Gods have a strange humour.

LAIS. I have no place in my heart, now, for death
Or disillusion.

[*She moves down to* MYRON, *taking his hand.*

Come !

MEDEA. You will have your way,
You children, and the salt of our experience
Savours your food of love only too late.
But I have brought trouble enough in the path
The Fates marked out for me. I will speed your
love
In safety. I have power.

LAIS (*alarmed*). I will not have it !
Your black power—help or hinder—I will not
have it !

MEDEA. Think—to keep you from harm ; to hold him
faithful.

LAIS. I know my own strength. When that fails
I am content to fail also.

MYRON. And I
Swear that you shall not fail. (MEDEA *laughs*.)
Come, we will go together
On our own quest.

LAIS (*looking at him, happily*). On our own quest.

[*They go off L., hand in hand, taking no notice of anyone
else.*

CLEANTHES. And I
Have——certain arrangements to make.

[*He turns to follow* MYRON *and* LAIS. MEDEA *stops him.*

MEDEA. Cleanthes !

CLEANTHES (*turning*). Well ?

MEDEA. Those two shall go in safety.

CLEANTHES. When I am dead, and when my power is
dead—if they are not dead first, which is unlikely.

MEDEA. I tell you they shall go in safety.

CLEANTHES (*making a show of defiance, though afraid*). And I say they shall die.

MEDEA (*taking a step or two towards him*). Do you know what I can do to you?

CLEANTHES (*shrinking back, fearfully*). Ah!

MEDEA. I can make your days and your nights terrible. I can make your nights so terrible that you will never dare bring their memory to the next sun.

CLEANTHES (*crying out in terror*). No! Leave me alone! Do not rack me! I—I will do what you ask. The girl shall go.

MEDEA. One thought otherwise, and I will twist you, body and soul—like this.

[*She throws out her hands towards him. He screams and drops on his knees.*

CLEANTHES. Aaah!

MEDEA. Now go.

[CLEANTHES *scrambles to his feet and, crouching, backs off L. The wind moans again, creaking the timbers of " Argo."* MEDEA *turns towards the last of the sunset, which lights her with* JASON *and " Argo." She speaks sadly, calm again.*

Come, spirits of storm, over unquiet seas
    To drive adown the distances, away,
All lingering memory, leaving only peace
    Here at the close of day.

Harden, O desolate heart, over the pain
    That will not otherwise be satiate.
In no such longing would I burn again
    As bowed my back to Fate,

But, drained of fury and love alike, would be
    Like one who dwells in some immaculate star,
Unmoved by time and chance, inexorably
    Calm as the high gods are.

[*She drops to her knees, her head bowed. The other* WOMEN *watch her in silence for a moment.*

RHEA. There is no more to be told. It is time for us to go.

[RHEA, AGLAIA, SEMELE, PHRYNE, ACANTHA, CALLIR-
RHOE, DORIS, IRIS *and* LALAGE *back off downstage* R.
in a group, slowly and silently, still looking towards MEDEA.
The wind rises. MEDEA, *crouching, and* JASON, *leaning
against the stem of "* Argo," *remain still for a moment. Then*
MEDEA *looks up towards* JASON.

MEDEA. There are other quests.

JASON (*wearily*). One—over the Styx.

MEDEA. No—in life. Life is not over. I can renew you,
Jason, as I renewed old Ægeus.

JASON. Through you I am childless. (*He turns towards
her.*)

MEDEA (*holding out her arms to him*). I say I can give you
back your youth—and I am yet beautiful. Would you
have another son?

JASON. I will have no more and no less than death.

[*He turns again to his original position, clinging to the
stem of "* Argo." MEDEA *again bows her head on her arms.
The storm increases. The Curtains close. Music, with storm
sounds continued. Immediately* AGLAIA, SEMELE, PHRYNE,
ACANTHA, CALLIRRHOE, DORIS, IRIS *and* LALAGE *enter*
R. *before the Curtain, making a group* C. *Some of them
carry lighted lanterns. The music and storm sounds fade down.*

AGLAIA.   The years pass, and the praise
                  Of men is an empty thing;

SEMELE.   And the unrelenting days
                  No more their gold may bring.

PHRYNE.   Why should we speak in blame
                  Of that which is past and gone?

ACANTHA.   For man has fame and shame,
                  Noon and midnight in one.

THE RIBS OF ARGO

CALLIRRHOE.   Man fares at the bidding of heaven
        In quest of the gold and the high ;

DORIS.   But alas ! for the loaf without leaven,
        Alas ! for the hope slipped by

IRIS.   Through the crowd of the moments
        thronging,
        The laugh and the lover's breath,

LALAGE.   To the cold stone grief of longing
        And the wild lone end of death.

AGLAIA.   Oh bitter the wrath that is brewed
        In the bowl of the world's praise ;

SEMELE.   And cunning the snares that are strewed
        O'er the track of a man's days.

PHRYNE.   Life, large-handed, will pour
        Her gifts on him who attains ;

ACANTHA.   But death has another score
        And the dark with the gold remains.

CALLIRRHOE.   Great are the gods, and know
        How hardly the best is won,

DORIS.   Yet will they laugh as we go
        Toward night from the known sun.

IRIS.   The skeins are tangled and snapped
        In the bony hands of Fate ;

LALAGE.   New meaning in meaning is wrapped,
        And the last is revealed—too late.

[*The music and storm sounds grow louder. The* WOMEN
*make a frightened group, clinging together. There is a great
burst of wind and a mighty crash. The Curtains open. The*

stage is in darkness now, the only light coming from the WOMEN'S *lanterns. They move slowly, in attitudes of horror, a little upstage, throwing the light of their lanterns on* JASON *who is lying dead, the stem of "Argo" fallen across his body.* MEDEA *is standing erect and still, her hair blown about by the wind. A moment's pause, the music continuing, rising with the storm.*

SLOW CURTAIN.

T. B. MORRIS

Rain In Majorca

A Play in One Act

LONDON
FREDERICK MULLER LTD.
29 Great James Street, W.C.1

FIRST PUBLISHED BY FREDERICK MULLER, LTD.
IN 1948
PRINTED IN GREAT BRITAIN BY WYMAN & SONS LTD.
LONDON, READING AND FAKENHAM

Rain in Majorca was first presented by the Warwick Road Church Players of Coventry in the Coventry Drama Festival at the Little Theatre on 23rd June, 1944, where it won the drama section and the new play prize, with the following cast :

Frédéric Chopin	.. .. ..	JOHN BARNFATHER
George Sand	.. .. ..	JOY FLANDERS
Maurice ..	.. .. ..	DOUGLAS GRIFFITHS
Solange ..	.. .. ..	SHEILA GEEN
Maria Antonia	.. .. ..	ANN WHETSTONE
Josefa ..	.. .. ..	PHYLLIS WILLISON
Lolona ..	.. .. ..	MARJORIE HANCOX
The Sacristan	.. .. ..	GEORGE CHERRY

The pianist was FREDERIC JUKES, A.R.C.O., L.R.A.M.
The play produced by ALBERT WHETSTONE.

THE CHARACTERS

FRÉDÉRIC CHOPIN. (28).

GEORGE SAND (*Amandine Aurore Dudevant*). (34).

MAURICE. (15).
SOLANGE. (10). } *George Sand's children.*

MARIA ANTONIA, *an old drudge, " housekeeper " at the monastery.*

JOSEFA.
LOLONA. } *peasant women.*

THE SACRISTAN.

THE SCENE

Chopin's cell in the deserted Carthusian monastery of Valldemosa, Majorca, late on a night of January, 1839.

SETTING AND PRODUCTION NOTES

Chopin himself, describing his cell, wrote " the shape of a tall coffin, with an enormous dusty vaulting, a small window, outside the window orange trees, palms, and cypresses, opposite the window my bed on rollers under a Moorish filigree rosette. Beside the bed is a square table for writing . . . and on it a leaden candlestick with a candle, the works of Bach, and my own manuscripts."

As his piano is not mentioned, and he had a local piano before his own arrived, this was presumably in another of the three cells which the party occupied, but for the purposes of stage presentation it is suggested that the setting should be adapted somewhat as follows : preferably stone walls, though a curtain setting may be used. The " fourth wall " is one of the long walls of the oblong cell, so that the door from outside is C.R., a square-topped doorway. Below this is a small square window. Upstage L. there is an inner door giving on to a corridor. The doors and window should be set in a considerable thickness of stone wall. In the downstage L. corner there is a small upright piano, set a little obliquely with its upstage end nearest the L. wall, so that, while the face of the composer is not hidden from the audience, his hands and the face of the instrument (which was a Pleyel) are not clearly seen. The back of the piano might be masked by a slightly projecting curtain or screen, or by a piece of vivid material thrown carelessly across it. There is a stool before the piano and a mass of manuscript music on it. Near it, at the upstage end, is a tall standard candlestick with a great candle of religious type. This might effectively be used to suggest the illumination, so that a pool of light is thrown about the piano and the rest of the cell is shadowy except when Chopin lights his table candle and other characters enter with lights. Backstage C. is a long dark chest, with a vase or two and a draping of rich bright material to provide a note of colour and suggest the influence of George Sand. Above this is a long oblong painting dark with age. To R. of the chest and a little downstage of it is a tall carved arm-chair of elaborate Spanish religious type. Downstage R. is a square table, with a metal candlestick, inkstand, quill and more manuscripts. A wooden chair is above the table, facing down to the audience, and other wooden chairs *ad lib*. The furniture, except the arm-chair, should be crude and heavy. Floor coverings should be grass mats or old sheepskins.

Where possible an effective addition to the setting would be another window backstage, giving a garden view such as Chopin describes, or alternatively (and even more effectively) a few ancient and twisted olive-trees, seen occasionally and weirdly as the moon breaks through heavy clouds. Dimming apparatus will be essential for this effect.

Unless a really good pianist is available, either to play the part of Chopin or (as was done in the original production) to provide the musical effects on another piano offstage, it is suggested that suitable gramophone records should be used for the music, except for the reiterated passages during the imagined composition, which must be played on a piano, either by the actor playing Chopin or by someone offstage L. If the pianist is offstage the actor's movements must be carefully timed with the music. (In the original production this was done by an electric switch on Chopin's piano keyboard, operating a bulb on the piano of the actual pianist). The piece at the beginning of the play may be anything of Chopin's composition before the date of the play. The later piece, which he plays partly during the play and more fully at the end, is the " Raindrops " *Prelude in D Flat* (one recording of which is Columbia L.1804).

The following compromise may be made in regard to accents : Chopin, a Pole, never thoroughly at home with French, but fluent with German, should speak with a slightly guttural accent throughout, except when he is alone and talking to himself. He should express some difficulty in speaking to the Peasants, Maria and the Sacristan, with hesitations over certain words, as it is imagined that he would address them in Spanish. For the same reason George Sand should speak to Maria and the Sacristan with a slight exaggeration of the French manner and a French accent, also with a little difficulty. She should lose these characteristics when speaking to Chopin, Maurice and Solange. The Peasants, Maria and the Sacristan, presumed to speak only Spanish, should speak naturally throughout.

The story of the composition of the *Prelude in D Flat* on which the play is based is contained in George Sand's *Histoire de ma Vie*, and, while a certain licence has been taken, the characters of Chopin and George Sand have been rendered as truly as is possible when two such personalities have to be dealt with in brief and from a mass of very conflicting records. The characters and actions of the children are sketched from later records of their lives and the parts they played in the separation of Sand and Chopin seven years later.

RAIN IN MAJORCA

After a moment's music in a dark theatre, the Curtain rises to reveal CHOPIN *playing the piano. He is twenty-eight, delicately built, elegantly dressed and fastidious. Pale, haggard, obviously ill, he is in a state of considerable nervous tension and his hair is dishevelled. It is a stormy night. Wind and heavy rain are heard at frequent intervals throughout the play, especially when the door R. is open. For a moment* CHOPIN *continues to play, now and again glancing fearfully over his shoulder.*

CHOPIN (*as he plays*). Shadows . . . shadows . . . Oh God, this place ! How I have grown to loathe it—to fear it ! . . . Haunted ! . . . (*Pause, shuddering, then in a more urgent tone.*) Why doesn't she return ?

[*A face has been pressed to the window. Now the door R. is quietly unlatched and the door opens slowly a little way. Louder storm noises warn* CHOPIN *of this.*

Ah-h-h !

[*He screams, sweeping his hands across the keys in a shattering discord, swinging round on his stool and staring in terror at the door, which is suddenly closed. He springs across the room and snatches the door open wide, desperately, fighting for breath. The light of a lantern is seen outside.*

Who's there ? Who are you ? Ah !

[*He makes a grab and drags in* LOLONA, *a peasant girl, who screams.* JOSEFA, *an older peasant woman, comes hurriedly into the doorway. She carries a lantern. Both women have head-shawls against the weather.*

JOSEFA (*placidly*). It's all right, señor. We meant no harm——

217

CHOPIN (*unsuccessfully fighting for control*). You—you disturb me! (*Petulantly.*) Am I not distracted enough by this damned island and all in it? Am I to have no privacy to eat my own soul? Am I to be flayed alive by these endless interruptions?

[*He begins to cough, staggering to the chest to support himself.* LOLONA *is frightened, but* JOSEFA *expresses a kindly concern.*

JOSEFA. You are ill, señor. You should be resting—not working here at your music so late of nights. Even a dumb beast should not be made to work when it is sick.

CHOPIN (*with difficulty*). We are all beasts—all. There is crawling evil everywhere. Everywhere—in our souls—clinging and crawling. Beasts—(*with bitter triumph*) but I am not dumb—no, I am not dumb. (*Suspiciously.*) What are you doing here?

JOSEFA. Your music, señor—it is of the angels——

CHOPIN (*derisively*). Angels—ha!

JOSEFA. We came to the monastery for blessing——

[*She pauses, timidly.* CHOPIN *has recovered a little.*

CHOPIN. And who is here to bless you? (*Ironically.*) Do you think my blessing will be of any use? Or the sacristan's?

JOSEFA (*gently*). We came for the blessing that a good place will give. There were holy monks here, and their blessings remain——

CHOPIN (*uneasily*). Their ghosts remain——

[LOLONA *crosses herself, nervously.*

JOSEFA. Lolona here, poor little one—my daughter, señor, and a good girl—she has been married for two years and she has no son. Think of that, señor. Two years—it is a long time. She has wept much for that, and is afraid her husband will beat her more. So we came to Valldemosa to pray to Our Lady in the old chapel here—and the storm caught us. (CHOPIN *is coughing again.*) Ah ! You must be very ill——

LOLONA (*nervously*). Is it catching ?

JOSEFA. Be quiet, child. You must not say these things to the kind señor who makes such beautiful music. (*To* CHOPIN.) They say you have come from a long way off to make your music here——

CHOPIN (*bitterly*). And shall stay. As well be on the moon as try to get anywhere from here. The torrents make the roads. The avalanches keep them in repair. There are no boats will dare the storms, and, if there were, they'd want them filled with their accursed pigs. Pigs, pigs, pigs—everywhere !

[MARIA ANTONIA, *a vicious, slatternly woman, enters abruptly* L., *carrying a bowl of milk and a candle.*

MARIA (*truculently*). Ay—pigs, pigs, pigs, pigs ! Good creatures that pay for their keep—and food for Christians. Food for *Christians*, I say. (*Banging down the bowl on the chest and turning to* JOSEFA.) And what may you want ?

JOSEFA. We came to get a blessing for my girl here, who has no son.

MARIA. Sons ! She'll find them something other than blessings before she's done with them. Begone with you, and don't come hanging about here. There are too many thieves about——

LOLONA. Thieves ! Oh, Mother—hear what she says——

JOSEFA (*indignantly*). Thieves, indeed ! The good saints put a bridle on your tongue——

MARIA (*advancing on* JOSEFA). So—a bridle ? And do you think that I, Maria Antonia, am the one to take such insolence from a common beggar ?

CHOPIN (*agitated*). Quiet ! Quiet ! Oh God, will nothing spare my nerves ? How may a man work in such a kitchen of hell ? The wind—the storm—clamour,

clamour, clamour ! (*Taking up the bowl, looking at it with distaste, then thrusting it at* MARIA.) This is dirty again.

MARIA. It is not !

CHOPIN. How often have I told you I'll not have your filthy ways ? See, the marks of your fingers in grime——

MARIA. Get that woman of yours to do your work for you.

CHOPIN. Quiet ! It is enough to have to drink goat's milk—pah !—without your filthy hands to poison it.

MARIA. Where is she now, that woman ? Tell me that. Gadding off so late at night when decent folk should be sleeping—(*Rounding on* JOSEFA.) Ay, and you, too. (*To* CHOPIN.) And taking that boy of hers along to catch his death o' this weather. Let her do your work, I say. If she can be your lover, she can be your wet-nurse, too.

CHOPIN (*furiously*). Stop your insolence ! Here—take this ! Empty it and wash it ! Wash it carefully before you dare bring it again——

MARIA (*insolently, not moving*). I'm not for the ordering of any who come here living in sin, with a devil's curse on them——

[CHOPIN *hurls the bowl across the room through the open door L., where it is heard to smash against the wall.* JOSEFA *starts.* LOLONA *screams.* MARIA *cackles derisively.* CHOPIN *exhausted by his anger, begins another fit of coughing, holding a handkerchief to his mouth and collapsing on to the chest.* MARIA *continues rapidly*:

Ay, smash a good basin you'll likely not replace nearer than Barcelona ! You fine gentlemen who think the world made for your dirty work ! (*To* JOSEFA.) Look, there's blood on his kerchief. (JOSEFA *and* LOLONA *are frightened.*) He's in a consumption. That's why good Señor Gomez turned him and his woman out of Palma, so that they had to come here—ay, and burned all their bedding after them for fear of the infection——

JOSEFA.
LOLONA. } Infection ! (*They back away.*)

MARIA. They've brought a curse to this place, those two. Not once have they been to Mass—to confession. (*Advancing on* JOSEFA *and* LOLONA, *who retreat before her.*) Why, I ask you, have we had such weather here this winter—who can remember it as bad ? It is because of this one and his woman and the devils they bring. Ay, because of that ! And I'll tell you something : she wears trousers like a man—shameless for all to see !— and the smoking of her tobacco would shame a chimney. (*Urgently.*) Go—go quickly, or you will catch the consumption and cough and die—and that child you want will be born with no lungs.

LOLONA (*terrified*). Mother !

JOSEFA (*crossing herself*). Our Lady preserve us ! }

    [LOLONA *grabs open the door R. They back off hastily, taking the lantern.* MARIA *calls maliciously after them.*

MARIA. And don't let me catch you prowling here again. Children, indeed ! Looking for what you can steal, more likely. (*She slams the door and returns to* CHOPIN.) A fine one you are to drag here and live in a holy monastery ! I wonder the old monks don't rise against you. They are here—(*pushing her face close to his*) in the vaults and passages and dark corners—ay, and in the very air. Listen to their ghost-fingers on the roof —tap, tap, tap !

CHOPIN (*weak and fearful*). Go—go away——

MARIA. Breaking good basins—wasting the goat's milk— daring to accuse me of dirt—huh ! (*Spits.*) I shall have something to say to that fancy woman of yours when she comes back, I promise you—*if* she comes back——

CHOPIN. She should be here——

MARIA. She's dead, as like as not, and that boy with her. Fallen down some ravine, I don't doubt. The Devil takes his own—ay, he takes his own.

[*She goes off, cackling maliciously, taking her candle, slamming the L. door.* CHOPIN *crouches against the wall.*

CHOPIN. Dead—dead fingers beat—beat, beat, beat——

[*He tries to pull himself together, staggering to the table, dropping on to the chair, burying his face in his hands. The raindrops continue to beat on the roof.* CHOPIN *again glances fearfully over his shoulder.*

Ghosts in the shadows—ah !

[*Taking the candle from the table, he lights it at the large candle, his hands shaking, then returns to the table, sitting again, his fingers tormenting his hair.*

Beat—beat—beat. Icy drops beating on my heart——

[*His hand begins to beat a measure. Inspiration comes to him. Still terrified, and glancing uneasily about, he snatches the quill and begins to scrawl on manuscript paper.*

Another prelude—I must finish them. Must. I must have money. Pleyel jews me—Probst and Schlesinger cheat me. Money I must have. The cost of this place —the cost of this wretched piano through the Customs, five hundred francs—damn them for robbers ! They all rob me, as they rob my Poland——

[*He closes his eyes, wearily, pressing his fingers over them, then attacks his work again, feverishly.*

God, my head's like a fire ! . . . Prelude—key of D Flat—a sustained throbbing——

[*The fingers of his left hand work as he writes, as if hammering keys. He springs up suddenly, taking his manuscript, quill and ink to the piano, then begins to tap out passages of his " Prelude in D Flat," repeating, altering, testing them, at times gentle and exquisite, but often passionate, harsh, terrified. The music, however, is only fragmentary as yet.*

There shall be monks—their ghosts are everywhere, as the old woman said—they are in procession—hooded skeletons—in the hollow cloister. Ghosts—ghosts—tapping—tapping—tapping——

[*He plays a few bars from the procession music of the middle section of the piece, repeating, altering, testing as before.* SOLANGE, *a pretty, high-spirited and often intractable girl of ten, enters quietly L., carrying a book. She sees he is working and goes to the arm-chair, sitting. For a few moments she tries to read, but her glances at* CHOPIN *and at the door R. become more frequent. Finally she can contain her uneasiness no longer. She drops the book and goes to* CHOPIN, *touching his arm. He starts, then, seeing who she is, smiles at her. A great affection exists between them, and she is a privileged interrupter.*

Ah—Solange, dear. I didn't hear you come. You should be in bed.

SOLANGE (*gravely, rather grown up*). Mama—she hasn't come back, nor Maurice.

CHOPIN (*anxiously, his eyes straying to the door R.*). No. Not yet. (*Trying to reassure her.*) But they'll come soon, my dear—soon.

SOLANGE. They've never been so late before. And it's so wet outside, and—I'm frightened here, all alone in this big place.

CHOPIN. Don't be frightened. And you're not alone. I'm here.

SOLANGE. But you're frightened, too. I know you are. All the dark stone passages, and the empty rooms locked up. You are frightened of them, aren't you?

CHOPIN (*making an effort to be gay*). I? Oh, no——

SOLANGE. And aren't you worried about Mama and Maurice—but you don't love Maurice, do you?

[*Chopin gives her a quick look, then evades the question.*

CHOPIN (*lightly*). There's only one thing I'm really afraid of.

SOLANGE. What's that?

CHOPIN. All those horrid little black pigs that go scamper, scamper all over the island—like this.

[*He illustrates, on the high notes of the piano, with squeaks.* SOLANGE *laughs.*

SOLANGE. But they're dear little black pigs. Only their mamas are funny——

CHOPIN. Their mamas—like this.

[*He illustrates, on the lower notes, with grunts.* SOLANGE *is delighted.*

But I see so many of them that I'm afraid I shall grow like them. And that wouldn't be pretty, would it?

SOLANGE (*reproachfully*). Now you're making fun of me, and I'm not a baby. I'm nearly grown up.

CHOPIN. Yes—very nearly.

SOLANGE. When I'm quite grown up, I shall write famous books like Mama does, *and* play the piano like you do.

CHOPIN. Then you'll be two famous people in one. And half the world will say : " If only Mademoiselle Solange didn't write books, she'd play the piano divinely." And the other half will say : " If only Mademoiselle Solange didn't play the piano, she'd write such beautiful books."

[*They laugh.*

SOLANGE. I wish I could play your piano.

CHOPIN. So you shall—for a moment. And then you must let me work.

[*He stands her in front of him, and helps her to play a gay little piece, doing most of it himself.*

SOLANGE (*delighted*). We did that beautifully, didn't we?

CHOPIN. Beautifully.*

[SOLANGE *moves away, then turns to* CHOPIN *suddenly, anxious again.*

SOLANGE. You're sure Mama will soon be here?

CHOPIN (*turning his face downstage so that she shall not see the fear in his eyes*). Oh yes, very soon. (*Controlling himself, smiling at her.*) Any moment now, I expect. And don't you think it would be good for Mademoiselle Solange to go to bed?

SOLANGE (*firmly*). No, not yet. But I won't disturb you any more. I'll just sit here and listen.

[CHOPIN *kisses her forehead. She returns to the arm-chair. He waves to her playfully, then begins his own work again, soon forgetting all about her. After a moment there is a gentle tapping on the door R.* SOLANGE *looks R., but* CHOPIN *does not hear it, nor the louder storm noises as the door is opened. The* SACRISTAN *enters, diffidently. He wears a wet cloak and hat, and carries a lantern. He places the hat and lantern carefully on the floor, spits respectfully outside, and closes the door quietly.*

SACRISTAN. Do not let me disturb you, señor. I come only to listen. Ah, the little señorita not yet in bed? Good evening, Señorita Solange.

SOLANGE (*crisply*). Good evening, Sacristan.

[CHOPIN *turns, looking at the* SACRISTAN *without speaking, then returns to his work, repeating passages, scrawling on his manuscript, through the following lines, of which he takes no notice whatever. The* SACRISTAN *sits on the chair above the table and begins to talk at* CHOPIN's *back.*

* *Alternatively.* SOLANGE *sits at the piano and plays a little piece of Chopin's, haltingly as a child would. Then she says :* " Now you play it." CHOPIN *plays the same piece exquisitely.* SOLANGE *says, ruefully :* " Oh ! " *and looks downcast for a moment.* CHOPIN *pats her shoulder and she smiles again.*

SACRISTAN. It is good to listen, I say, and so I tell all my friends. He who listens most hears most. (*Chuckles.*) And such music as the señor's ! Ah, it marches, it marches ! Every day when I meet the señora in the cloisters, I ask : " And how goes the music ? " And always she will answer : " The poor little one, he is ill. He cannot work. His work sleeps, and he cannot sleep." So she will tell me, but I know better than that. I have an ear for music, for my grandfather—as I have doubtless told you, for I tell everyone—was a notable player on the guitar. Known through all Spain, my grandfather was, from Ronda to Barcelona. Ah, it is a good instrument, the guitar. The señor should try it. He would not have to pay so many gold pieces to get a guitar through the Customs—aha, no !

[He chuckles gently, and pauses while he takes snuff.

That Maria Antonia, the shiftless one, she is in a fierce rage and muttering to herself like a witch. The señor has said something she does not like. It is easy to say things a woman does not like. (*Chuckling again, rising.*) Well, time passes, and I must finish my round. It doesn't matter—now, but we must keep up the old customs. (*Taking a few steps R., then turning.*) Good night, señor ! I have enjoyed the music and our little chat. It is good to exchange views with another man of culture. God be with you, and with you, Señorita Solange.

[He takes up his hat, adjusts it carefully, takes his lantern, opens the door R., spits respectfully outside, and goes off, closing the door gently behind him. CHOPIN'S *work is increasingly feverish. Sometimes he coughs, or rests his head on his hands, then attacks the work again.* SOLANGE, *tired of sitting still, fidgets a little, glances at* CHOPIN *then uneasily R., and finally creeps off L. without speaking. At the sound of the door closing behind her* CHOPIN *starts. Suddenly he jumps up, pacing, beating out a rhythm with one hand on the other palm.*

CHOPIN. Drop after drop—beating—beating—— (*Coming to himself.*) It is late. God ! where are they ?

[CHOPIN *runs to the door R., throwing it open. His hair and cravat are blown by the wind as he stands staring out into the darkness.*

They're dead ! They must be dead ! She has never left me for so long. Darkness—all darkness ! And I'm alone in this damned, damned island !

[*He starts a fit of coughing and staggers back to the arm-chair, huddling in it, leaving the door open. The wind increases, flickering the candle-flames and blowing dead leaves into the room.* CHOPIN *bursts into tears.*

All my life searching—never finding . . . Poland lost— Marie lost . . . And now—alone——

[*Dragging himself up, he returns to his piano, playing a part of the prelude in a more completed form against the storm noises, hysterically.* GEORGE SAND *enters R. She is thirty-four, small, olive-skinned, with bobbed dark hair reaching to her shoulders, and beautiful dark eyes. She wears a picturesque cloak, man's trousers and a bright blouse. Her appearance is vital, passionate, Gypsy-like, attractively untidy, in vivid contrast with* CHOPIN'S. *She carries a large basket filled with purchases, is wet, storm-beaten, utterly exhausted. Her arm is about* MAURICE, *a boy of fifteen, who, also wet and tired, enters with her. He carries a lantern. For an instant* GEORGE *leans against the doorpost, then reacts to the music, delighted, raising her head, with an imperative gesture to* MAURICE *to be quiet. They listen for a moment, then* MAURICE *shrugs and, closing the door, goes to the nearest chair, throwing himself upon it, putting his lantern on the floor.* CHOPIN *stiffens, stops playing, turns slowly, dazed, gaping at them as if groping for recognition.*

Ah ! So you are dead ? You are ghosts. I knew you were dead——

GEORGE (*her fatigue momentarily forgotten, urgently*). Why do you stop playing. Go on, go on ! It is exquisite !

CHOPIN (*strangely*). The drops beat on my heart as I drowned in a storm of sorrow . . . I play to ghosts— and you are ghosts——

GEORGE (*moving C., wearily*). No, Frédéric, we are not ghosts. (*She puts down her basket and drops on to the chest with a little laugh.*) Not dead—but nearly. Oh, my friend, the torrents ! Floods everywhere, and the roads all but impassable. And such blackness ! Times and times the carriage was nearly over a precipice, and then the driver—that son of a pig !—deserted us and we have had to walk. We have walked three whole leagues —ah-h-h !

MAURICE (*disgusted*). And taken six hours to do it. (*Viciously, to* CHOPIN.) And much you care !

GEORGE (*at once concerned for* MAURICE, *her favourite child*). Ah, Maurice ! You are wet through. Go and take off your clothes at once, and I'll have Maria heat some milk.

MAURICE (*sulkily*). Not goat's milk—I hate the stuff ! Keep that for him. (*He indicates* CHOPIN.) I'll have some wine.

[*He rises, takes up the lantern, and moves stiffly towards L., stopping to regard* CHOPIN *with antagonism.*

You never stirred a foot to look for us. Is that all your feeling for my mother ?

GEORGE. That will do, Maurice.

[CHOPIN *looks at* MAURICE *without replying. He dislikes* MAURICE, *but is in no condition to argue with him at the moment. He therefore ignores the boy and turns again to* GEORGE. MAURICE *goes off L., scornfully, taking the lantern.* CHOPIN *goes to* GEORGE, *dropping on to the chest beside her.*

CHOPIN. So—you are not dead ?

GEORGE (*stroking down his ruffled hair, treating him as a child*). Of course we are not dead, little one. Am I to be killed by a storm ? Not I, my friend, I adore storms ! But, dear God, I am tired.

CHOPIN (*petulantly, rising*). You leave me so long alone——

[GEORGE *rises, tossing off her cloak. She is almost dropping with fatigue, and is forced to sit again, this time in the arm-chair.*

GEORGE. My feet—they are two fiery hells . . . The *stones* of Majorca ! . . . Alone ? Of course I leave you alone. You must be alone for your composition. Do not I, an artist, recognize an artist's needs ? Besides, I must go to Palma to do the shopping—weather or no weather. We must eat, and we do not want eternally to eat pigmeat and garlic and lean hens with fleas on them and rancid oil. But it has been terrible to-day— but terrible !

CHOPIN (*concerned with himself*). I do not compose better alone. I'm terrified of this place. It's like a stone coffin in a hall of the dead.

GEORGE. Ah ! But you are inspired when you are terrified. I know you.

CHOPIN. No, no ! I shall never do any real work here. Oh, I wish to God we could get away !

GEORGE. So we shall—in the spring.

CHOPIN. The spring ? There will never be any more spring ! And I came south after the sun. Why didn't we go to Italy—Spain—anywhere except this accursed, cold, wet Majorca ?

[GEORGE *pulls herself together, rises again and goes to* CHOPIN, *putting an arm round him, drawing him to the arm-chair and making him sit, soothing him.*

GEORGE. There, little one, calm yourself ! You know very well—as I've reminded you a thousand times— that we came here because you wished it ; because you didn't wish to meet your friends on such a journey with me. You would have met someone, but certainly, if we had gone to Italy or stayed in Spain. Besides, you liked Majorca well enough when the sun shone.

CHOPIN. You wanted to come here because it was new to you—made copy for your books. Everything—every-thing must make copy for your books. And now you blame me.

GEORGE. I blame no one. I do not complain, though I have worn the shoes nearly off my feet, and destroyed myself quite in that weather. But I tell you we came here because you wished to avoid scandal. You know you did, Frédéric. I never mind what anyone says, but you can't bear the thought of it.

CHOPIN (*springing up, irritably*). Pah ! This place——

GEORGE (*interrupting, on edge but trying to keep her temper*). Am I to blame that there is no decent hotel in the island ; that we were driven out of Palma ?

CHOPIN (*bitterly*). Ah ! It comes back to blame of me— my cough that frightened them ; that made them drive us out. Why don't you leave me here to rot alone ?

GEORGE. Frédéric ! You mustn't speak like this ! I do not desert my friends. (*Half to herself.*) Let them say what they will—it is they who desert me. (*Making another effort.*) Come ! Play me your new piece. That will cure my tiredness——

CHOPIN (*touched*). Forgive me ! My own troubles drive me always to forgetting yours. You are tired, and wet, and hungry I expect, and I—I'm full as usual of my own grievances.

GEORGE (*caressing him again*). Of course, little one, as you should be. Genius must be full of grievances, or it will do no work. Come and play to me—then you must go to bed. It is too late for you to be up.

[*But* CHOPIN *is in no mood for coddling. He starts away, again irritable.*

CHOPIN. Damnation ! It is always the same—I am the invalid, the child, to be coddled and comforted ! Am I something less than a man and your lover, that you persist in playing at mothering me ?

GEORGE. Frédéric, Frédéric ! You drive me to distraction ! You are ill, and you make a detestably impossible patient——

CHOPIN. Detestable ! Yes, that is it ! Now it comes out ! You are tired of me—and I don't wonder. God ! I can't even finish these damned preludes and get money for this—(*bitterly*) honeymoon of ours.

GEORGE. Now you are deliberately hurting me. Money, money! What is it? Why do you let it trouble you? I can get it—I have told you I can get it. I've written again to that greedy editor, Buloz, and promised him my new novel soon if he pays at once. My pen is to spin out money to feed your music—for nothing but that, I've told you. You should not be troubled with these things——

CHOPIN (*impatiently*). You—oh, you to keep me! I'm smothered by this wrapping-up in wool!

[*He goes violently to the door R. again, throwing it open, letting in the storm and gusts of wind. His cravat and hair are blown about, and the candles flicker again.* GEORGE, *alarmed, runs to him.*

GEORGE. No, no! You'll catch your death——

[*She tries to drag him back into the room. He resists her, petulantly.*

CHOPIN. So much the better. I wish to God I'd never seen a piano! I wish to God I'd never been an artist! Why couldn't I have been a soldier and died in the defence of Poland? Then I'd have gloried, not suffered. Ah, there is no suffering like the pursuit of the impossible!

GEORGE (*coaxing again*). Died—no no! Come in—come, and close that door. You have done more for Poland than all her heroes, and will do more yet. And you do not pursue the impossible. You achieve perfection. You achieve, my friend, achieve! In all the world there are no piano compositions to equal yours. Liszt, even, is no more than your shadow. (*Sharply, as he takes no notice.*) Come in, I say! . . . *Frédéric!* Do you think I want to stay here all night? I'm tired, and I've hours of work to do yet, on my wretched pot-boiler for Buloz. (*Pleading.*) Be reasonable, my friend. (*Again sharply, alarmed.*) Do you hear me? Do you think I want you worse again? What will your friends say if I take your dead body back to France?

[CHOPIN *starts, horrified. He swings round, staring at* GEORGE, *who instantly regrets her words.*

No no! I did not mean that! But you exasperate me so.

CHOPIN (*brutally*). You need not concern yourself with my dead body. You can leave me behind, here. It's easier to desert a dead lover than a living one.

GEORGE (*tense*). What is this?

CHOPIN. Alfred de Musset was ill—though not so sick as I.

[*He strides abruptly across the room and goes off L., slamming the door.* GEORGE, *terribly hurt, stares after him for a moment.*

GEORGE (*to herself*). Alfred! Does no one ever blame *you*, Alfred, that this old tale sticks to me?

[*She leans her head against the doorpost and begins to cry, quietly, the wind blowing her hair. After a moment the* SACRISTAN *comes to the open door, fighting the storm.* GEORGE *takes no notice of him.*

SACRISTAN (*gently garrulous*). Señora—ah, señora, what is it? I saw the light, and I thought: "Ah, his door is open. His door should not be open, letting in the night air, which, as everyone knows, is deadly—especially when there is so much of it, and to one in his condition." So I told myself—and I know. The lungs are weak, that is it. I have had experience of that. Poor Brother Philip, his lungs were weak, too. So good and gentle, he was, and as kind to the little birds as Blessed Saint Francis himself.

[GEORGE *moves wearily down to the chair above the table, sitting, resting her head on her hands. The* SACRISTAN *spits respectfully outside, closes the door, carefully puts down his hat and lantern, and moves down to her, still talking.*

I buried him in the most peaceful corner of the cemetery. There is a great old olive-tree that reaches its branches above his grave.

GEORGE. Olive—ah, those old olives, writhen and tortured with their thousand years of living! They are things of hell—yet they are beautiful and wise. (*Interested, pursuing an idea.*) Olives—they saw the passion of Christ in Gethsemane, and they have ever since been tormented. That is it. I must remember that.

SACRISTAN. It is a beautiful thought. But the señora is full of beautiful thoughts. I sometimes think that the señora and the Señor Chopin are very nearly the most interesting people I have ever met—and I have met some, I can tell you. But what a pity—if I may venture to say so—that you are not married.

GEORGE (*jumping up, flashing at him*). Marriage—I am married already, and one husband is enough for any woman. Let me tell you that no one is justified in claiming ownership of another soul—as you men claim when you marry us.

SACRISTAN (*delighted to have found another opportunity for talk*). I? Oh, I have never claimed anything of the kind. But I see that we are about to have a very interesting discussion. If the señora will allow me, I will sit.

GEORGE (*amused, straddling over the chair above the table, leaning her arms on the back*). Lord help the man! Do you want me to tell you the story of my life?

SACRISTAN (*sitting*). That would indeed be interesting——

GEORGE. It would indeed be scandalous. (*Fumbling in the drawer of the table she produces a cigar, which she lights at the candle, smoking it expertly and contentedly.*) The proprieties, Monsieur le Sacristan, are the guiding principles of people without souls or true virtue.*

SACRISTAN (*shocked*). To smoke—if I may venture to say so, that is not a good habit for a lady.

GEORGE. But I'm not a lady. Of a certainty I've royal blood on one side, but on the other—oh dear! (*She*

---

* *If naked candles are not allowed on stage,* GEORGE *indicates the lantern and says:* " A light." *The* SACRISTAN, *shocked, opens his lantern and holds it for her to light her cigar, then again puts down the lantern and sits.*

laughs.) I'll not shock you. Let it suffice that I am not a lady, because I'm a far greater thing—a woman. And a woman should have the privileges of a man—cigars—career—lovers.

SACRISTAN. But——

GEORGE. Do not interrupt me. I tell always the most interesting things to those who do not interrupt. I have told the story of my life to everyone of consequence in France.

SACRISTAN. Then I am truly honoured, and I would remind the señora that I myself am not without consequence in Majorca. True, here at Valldemosa we are not what we were, but——

[*She blows a cloud of smoke over him, choking him, then goes on :*

GEORGE. My father's mother was a great lady. My own mother—ah ! Her past will not bear looking into. They were enemies, of course, and I had to live now with one and now with the other. My grandmother was of a stiffness—ah ! My mother—well, well ! I loved her only to annoy my grandmother. Picture to yourself the life of a young girl in such conditions——

SACRISTAN. I picture it.

GEORGE. I married the first man who came along. The wrong one, of course. He spent my money, and seduced my maid, and wrote a very rude letter for me to read after he was dead. I read it before—and left him.

SACRISTAN. Naturally, señora. (*Doubtfully.*) At least, I suppose——

GEORGE (*cutting him short*). I earned my own living in Paris. (*Rising.*) And I defy any man to say that the place I have made in the world is not as good as his. Moreover—mark this !—I have not neglected my children. They say of me—ah ! all sorts of things—but they cannot say I am not a good mother. (*Suddenly changing her manner.*) Why do I tell you this ?

SACRISTAN (*taken aback*). I—I haven't the least idea, señora.

GEORGE (*laughing*). Perhaps to prove that women are at least as good as men. No no, it is that I lack a confidant here. One cannot confide in a lover——

SACRISTAN. Not? But——

GEORGE. My good friend, whatever you do, never confide in your mistress. (*The* SACRISTAN *starts up, deeply shocked.*) Tell all your secrets to your laundrywoman, but never to your sweetheart——

SACRISTAN. But, señora—I assure you I have no sweetheart. I never have had. (*He spits on the floor.*) Ah, a million pardons! In the agitation of my thoughts I forget my manners.

GEORGE (*serious now, taking no notice of his words*). And one more thing. If your sweetheart should tell you that she no longer loves you, do not at once believe her and take another sweetheart. I did that—ah!—I have been hurt.

[*Brief pause.* GEORGE *is agitated. Then she continues, urgently:*

Go away—go! Leave me! I wish to have no more to say about it.

SACRISTAN (*surprised*). But, señora, we have scarcely begun——

[MAURICE *enters L., wearing a dressing-gown, unnoticed.*

GEORGE. We have finished. We have said too much. I have said too much. I always say too much. (*Throwing herself on the chair by the table.*) Alfred—Alfred! Why have I been so reminded of you?

SACRISTAN (*embarrassed*). I—I trust *I* have not reminded you of anyone . . . I will wish you good night, señora, and take myself off. Good night. (*He hastily takes up his hat and lantern and bows himself off R., seeing* MAURICE *as he goes.*) Ah, good night, Señor Maurice.

[*Neither* GEORGE *nor* MAURICE *reply. The* SACRISTAN *goes off R., closing the door after a last anxious glance back into the room.*

GEORGE (*to herself*). George Sand and Alfred de Musset —Alfred de Musset and George Sand . . . Yes, they would blame me. You were sick, Alfred, and I deserted you—that is what they say. Well, *they shall not say that of me this time.*

MAURICE. Mama! What is it? Why are you here talking to yourself? You're wet and tired, and you've had no food.

GEORGE (*vaguely*). What? (*Starting, as she realizes his presence.*) Oh, you, Maurice——

MAURICE (*sitting*). There's a fine mess in the corridor —a bowl of milk smashed all over the place. Chopin did that. And you should see Maria Antonia——

GEORGE (*rising*). Ah, my poor Frédéric! I had forgotten him—almost. Where is he?

MAURICE. Gone to the Devil, for all I care.

GEORGE. Maurice! How often am I to tell you that I will have Monsieur Chopin respected.

MAURICE. Respect? How can I respect him?

GEORGE. You are to regard him as your uncle.

[MAURICE *laughs derisively.* GEORGE *reacts, annoyed.* MAURICE *softens.*

MAURICE (*going to* GEORGE, *kissing her*). I'm sorry, Mama. But you must admit this is a queer position for me. All right for Solange—she's only a child—but——

GEORGE. That is enough——

MAURICE. If he were a man, I'd fight him. But he's no better than a girl, with his tears and his delicacy, his white gloves and essences—pah!

GEORGE (*sharply*). Maurice! (*Controlling herself, indulgent again.*) Silly boy! You yourself are only a child—

you have so much to learn. And I'll not quarrel with you.

[SOLANGE *runs on L., going to* GEORGE, *catching her dress.*

SOLANGE. Oh, Mama, what have you done to poor Uncle Frédéric?

GEORGE. Solange! I thought you were in bed long ago. And not even undressed! You know what I told you—if you want to be beautiful, you must go to bed early and have much sleep.

SOLANGE. I don't want to be beautiful. Beautiful ladies are vain and a nuisance—like Madame d'Agoult. I want only to be clever. Besides, *you* don't go to bed before dawn—and sometimes not then.

GEORGE. Because I must work to keep you children.

MAURICE. And this Chopin. You keep him, too.

GEORGE (*furious*). How dare you!

SOLANGE. He is wandering about the corridors like one of the ghosts. Why?

GEORGE. Do not ask questions about what is no concern of yours, Solange.

SOLANGE (*mutinously*). But this does concern me. I love him—ah, here he is!

[CHOPIN *enters L., calmer, and for the moment in one of his gentler moods. He goes to* GEORGE, *taking her hands, ignoring* SOLANGE *and* MAURICE.

CHOPIN. Forgive me! I should not have said what I did.

GEORGE (*smiling at him*). It hurt—but it is forgotten now. (*To* MAURICE *and* SOLANGE.) Go to bed children—at once. Good night.

[*She kisses* MAURICE *affectionately, patting his cheek to show that he is forgiven. Then she kisses* SOLANGE, *casually.* SOLANGE *goes to* CHOPIN, *who kisses her forehead.*

MAURICE (*nastily*). Mama—do you think that Chopin ought to kiss Solange ? (*They stare at him.*) As he is in a consumption, I mean.

[*Pause.*

SOLANGE. What does Maurice mean ?

GEORGE (*with an effort*). Nothing, child. Maurice is being naughty, and I shall give him an extra hour's lessons to-morrow to punish him. Now go, both of you.

MAURICE. But——

[GEORGE's *glance flashes fire at* MAURICE, *compelling his silence. He turns and stalks off L.* SOLANGE *follows him, turning at the door for a mutinous last word.*

SOLANGE. I shall kiss him as often as I like.

[*She goes off.* CHOPIN *and* GEORGE *look at each other in silence.*

CHOPIN (*wearily*). How that son of yours hates me.

GEORGE. Maurice is growing up. And already he understands—too much.

CHOPIN. About you and me. Naturally. What do you expect of a boy of fifteen (*meaningly*) and very well informed ? We should not have brought him—I told you that.

GEORGE (*obstinate but quiet, fighting to remain normal*). Frédéric —I will not be separated from my children. Not by anyone. So much of my independence I have already given up for them.

CHOPIN. Solange is a dear child.

GEORGE. You spoil her. She is naughty and self-willed —far naughtier than Maurice.

CHOPIN. No. Maurice has too much of his father in him. But Solange—I wish she were my child.

GEORGE (*flatly*). Well, she is not. And I will warn you again, Frédéric, that I will have no interference—none —in the affairs of my family. With that you have, and shall have, nothing to do. . . . I think, too, that what Maurice says, about your kissing Solange, is correct.

[CHOPIN *paces. It is now his turn to fight for control.*

CHOPIN. I never kiss her lips. (*Irritably.*) Do you think I've no consideration—no feelings—no sense of my own position?

GEORGE (*instantly sympathetic, forgetting her jealousy, a hand on his shoulder*). There there! It is forgotten, isn't it, my dear?

CHOPIN (*breaking away*). How can these things be forgotten? These germs of little hates and discomforts and faulty compromises—they spread and spread like a poison in the blood, killing self-respect, stifling ideals——

GEORGE. I do not stifle anyone's ideals.

CHOPIN. You do. You never understand me. You are not content to possess me as woman possesses a lover. You must needs obliterate me with your possessiveness —my mind—my thoughts——

GEORGE (*quietly*). Frédéric! You go too far.

CHOPIN. It is true. Did I ever pursue you? No. It was you who pursued me. In Liszt's honour I gave a party, you remember, and, when I was playing there, you came to me and kissed me before everyone . . . Oh, I suppose I promised more copy for you. It's true, isn't it, that you draw your portraits from your lovers? (*With a gesture of despair.*) Oh, I'm sorry—again sorry! Why do you goad me into saying these things? Why don't you leave me alone?

GEORGE (*still quietly*). That was unjust. I kissed you in homage—for your art. As for using you as copy—— (*Suddenly passionate, a torrent of words.*) Name of God! Have I not dedicated myself and my work to your art? You need me, you cannot exist without me, yet you resent what you call my possessiveness! Have I ever stood between you and your work, for a moment, for an instant? Ah, madman, can't you see what I do for you? And am I any ordinary woman to do this? I am not! I, too, am a genius! I am in letters what you are in music. You—you—oh, is woman forever to be bound like a slave to the triumphal car of man's intolerance ? Do you think I like writing sentimental pot-boilers—so many hours ; so many pages every day—for that Buloz, who breaks my back with his demands ? No. You should know that I have deeper ideas to pursue—I. There are books on life, the spirit, the better things, surging within me to be written. Yet, when I deny them, when I clip my aspirations for you, for my children, for money-making—ah ! you—you who should be sensitive and understanding, you accuse me of wanting to overwhelm and possess you utterly.

CHOPIN (*wearily*). I am wrong. I've grown bitter, and so I say these things. It is my life—my lungs—my work that lags—and this damned island.

[*He coughs.* GEORGE, *regarding him with sympathy again, continues more gently :*

GEORGE. Think of me sometimes before you think of yourself. All night long I must spin my webs of treacle for Buloz, because all day I must look to the house-keeping, the lessons of Maurice and Solange, and the watching of that dirty old hag, Maria Antonia——

[MARIA, *furious, bursts on L.*

MARIA. What is this I hear ?

GEORGE. Ah, so you were listening at the door again.

MARIA. Dirty—I ? Dirty ! That is once, twice I have been called dirty to-night. (*Pointing off L.*) Regard that mess. That is the bowl of good goat's milk I brought here for your pretty lover. He threw it there, and there it may stay until it stinks for all I care. Am I an honest woman, or what, to have bowls of milk thrown at my head ?

GEORGE. Go away, Maria. At some other time I will speak to you——

MARIA. At some other time—huh ! (*Spits.*) And who do you think you are, my fine lady ? I'll have no more from you—with your trousers and your tobacco and your lovers—bah ! Yes, I've heard of you. They say you take a new lover every six weeks.

GEORGE. Ah—liar ! ⎫

CHOPIN. How dare you ! ⎭

MARIA. In future you shall do your own sweeping and scrubbing, ay, and everything else. I'll not do it, and where else in this island will you find help ? Accursed of God, both of you ! (CHOPIN *is coughing again.*) Listen to him ! Soon he will cough up all his lungs, and then he will die——

GEORGE. No, no !

MARIA. —and, when he is dead, do you think we'll find him good Christian burial here—do you think that ? No—you may bury him like a dog or a suicide. I'll see you do. I'll stir up our people against you. Not one inch of good holy ground shall you have for him. You do not insult Maria Antonia for nothing. Dirty— huh ! *You* to call me dirty ! You two——

[GEORGE, *driven beyond endurance, moves quickly to* MARIA *and smacks her face, again and again, furiously.*

GEORGE. Stop your foul tongue, woman ! Let that teach you—and that ! And go, if you wish. We shall be well rid of you—lazy—dirty—prying old scandalmonger —and thief into the bargain——

MARIA (*frightened, backing off L. in a hurry*). Ah, Mother of God ! Saints protect me ! She is gone mad ! There are seven devils in her ! Oh—oh——

[GEORGE *drives* MARIA *off L., slams the door, returns to the arm-chair and collapses in it.* CHOPIN, *coughing, watches her. Pause.*

GEORGE (*quietly*). So ! I may sweep and scrub—as well as all the rest ? Well, the good God put twenty-four hours to every day—He should have made them thirty-six for me. Did we call this a honeymoon, Frédéric ?

CHOPIN (*dully*). You shall not suffer it. Go away and leave me here. I take too much from you. You can do without me.

GEORGE. But you cannot do without me, little one.

CHOPIN. What does that matter? I shall cough away my life in this island, as that old woman said—here among the ghosts—very soon. (*In terror.*) I shall never leave this place—never again see France—never, never again see Poland——

GEORGE (*springing up*). You shall, you shall! And I'll not leave you. They said I left de Musset when he was ill—de Musset who drove me from him and flaunted his other women—ah, my dear! They shall not say that about you——

CHOPIN. So it is only your pride—or your fear of what the world will say? There is no love——

GEORGE (*hurt, desolate*). Love? Oh, dear God! What has *that* love to do with us?

[*She looks at him for a moment, then goes to him, putting her hands on his shoulders, looking into his eyes.*
There is an old love in my heart——

CHOPIN. That de Musset. I know.

GEORGE. An old love in yours——

CHOPIN. No.

GEORGE. Yes! Yes, you weak fool—will you deny it? A love that happens once, and only once. The Polish girl who thought herself too high and proud for the poor composer. (CHOPIN *reacts.*) I've heard you cry her name from your dreams—Marie—Marie Wodzinska. (*Pause.*) So, we are equal. The best is no more for our giving, but—we need each other, Frédéric.

CHOPIN. Unhappy as we are—only to light small fires over the ashes of our hearts.

GEORGE. Are we on earth for no more than to be happy? My friend, you are a genius. Genius is always repressed, solitary, suffering, misunderstood. I tell you, if there is no conflict, no unhappiness, there is no work. We have something greater than happiness, you and I.

CHOPIN. Then I'm not great enough—nor strong enough to hold it. I cannot work.

GEORGE. But you do work ! Come and play me this new piece—now !

CHOPIN (*wearily*). Another prelude. I must finish them before I die. I've promised them. (*Bitterly.*) Then, if I remember to make no more promises, I can die in peace at my pleasure.

GEORGE (*sharply, snapping him out of his mood*). Attention, Frédéric ! You are not going to die. The angels do not want you—they make their own music in heaven, and they do not use the pianoforte. (*Inspired.*) Only you can make such music on earth, and you must stay here—for the world—and for me. Come, little one, play to me. Let me be the first to hear it all.

[*She leads* CHOPIN *to the piano. He begins to play. After a moment his bitterness leaves him and he becomes engrossed in his music, playing the " Prelude in D Flat " with great power, brilliantly. The storm sounds have died away.* GEORGE, *sitting in the arm-chair, watches him for a moment, entranced, then looks straight before her, speaking against the music.*

I am greedy for your music ! I am greedy for life—for all of life—for all experience ! Were I a painter, no colours would be rich enough. Were I a musician, I would exhaust the range and volume of the greatest orchestra. There shall be mud and flame and agony mixed with my purple of life. That is as it should be for the descendant of kings and courtesans.

[*She pauses for a moment, then rises, moving towards* CHOPIN, *speaking more gently.*

But you, my dear, you are different, fastidious. You concentrate upon the exquisite things, the delicate tones, the austere and immaculate. Yours is the limitation of chastity—mine the universal embrace of impulsive passion. See, then, how much we need each other !

[*Another pause.* CHOPIN, *inspired, continuing to play, has taken no notice.* GEORGE *goes on :*

No, my little Chopin, they shall not say of me again that I deserted a lover. (*Expanding to the music, possessive of it all, in a ringing voice.*) They shall say that I—*I* was your Muse ; that I made you live—for this !

[CHOPIN *goes on playing, lost to everything but the music. As the piece crashes into its most majestic chords*

THE CURTAIN FALLS